FROM THE AUTHOR OF
'BE A PMP ACE IN 30 DAYS'

300 Practice Questions for the PMP Exam

ROJI ABRAHAM, PMP

300 Practice Questions for the PMP Exam

Copyright © 2016 by Roji Abraham

ISBN-13: 978-1541012233

ISBN-10: 1541012232

Contents

Introduction

When I published my first book on the Project Management Professional (PMP) exam, 'Be a PMP Ace in 30 Days', my primary objective was to provide PMP test candidates with a well-defined process for exam preparation. The book was based on my personal journey to PMP certification and was specifically meant for those who had difficulties in narrowing down on the right resources or were struggling to create a study schedule they could adhere to. The book was very well received and in the days since its publishing, I received numerous 'thank-you' emails from people who had successfully passed the PMP Exam after following the guidelines in the book. If you haven't read 'Be a PMP Ace in 30 Days' yet, do check it out. It will ease your PMP exam preparation journey.

It was the success of 'Be a PMP Ace in 30 Days' that led me to believe that I could bring something else too of great value to PMP test aspirants – a concise and well written question-bank.

Every PMP test-taker will know that attempting practice questions and learning from them is crucial for succeeding in the real examination. The time I was prepared for the PMP Exam, one major issue I faced was that despite the presence of numerous websites that provided resources to aid PMP candidates with their exam preparation, it was difficult to come across reasonably priced good quality practice questions.

A more pertinent issue I encountered when I started using cheaper/free practice questions was that only a handful of them were of consistently high quality. Many of the practice questions I had spent time on were poorly framed or unintelligible. Occasionally, even the reasoning provided for an answer was inadequate or ambiguous which inadvertently made these practice questions a waste of time.

A third issue I faced was that, more often than not, the good quality practice questions I came across were in the 'Full-length Exam Format', or in other words, these questions were available only as a mixed set of 200 questions spread across all knowledge areas. This meant a student couldn't attempt these questions after studying each individual chapter, but instead, had to wait till he/she finished studying all knowledge areas of the PMP Exam, and then attempt the questions.

It was to address all these problems that I decided to focus my efforts into creating a value-for-money, high-quality question-bank that would contain practice questions sorted on knowledge areas

'300 Practice Questions for the PMP Exam' is the net result of my efforts. This book equips you with a wide variety of high-quality questions similar to what you are likely to encounter on the actual PMP Exam. Testing your knowledge using these questions and learning from them will surely propel you ahead in your quest for PMP success.

Thank you for purchasing this book and I wish you all the best for the PMP Exam!

Roji Abraham

The PMP Exam Format: An Overview

The PMP Exam contains 200 multiple-choice questions that are distributed across the 5 process groups of Initiating, Planning, Executing, Monitoring and Controlling, and Closing. While scoring is done on only 175 of these questions, it is not possible to identify the ones that are not graded and therefore a candidate will need to answer all questions without skipping any. There is no negative marking for wrong answers.

There are four answer choices provided with each question and of these four answer choices, only one answer choice is deemed correct (or is considered the best answer choice). There are mainly three categories of questions as follows:

1. **Knowledge Based Questions** – In questions of this type, a candidate is tested on his knowledge of the various project management processes, the tools and techniques used, and the various inputs or outputs of these processes.

2. **Formula Based Questions** – In questions of this type, a candidate will need to carry out some computation. The majority of formula based questions pertain to the knowledge areas of Cost Management and

Procurement Management. However, there are formula based questions from other knowledge areas too, though lesser in number.

3. **Scenario/Situation Based Questions** – Questions of this type test the ability of the candidate to apply theoretical knowledge in real-life project management situations. The test candidate will need to draw on his knowledge to choose the best option after carefully considering what is asked in the question. There are often intentionally misleading answer choices meant to confuse candidates in these questions and a key word such as 'except' or 'not' in the question could hold the vital clue in understanding the question.

Suggestions on How to Use This Book

The questions in this book are a healthy mix of all the three types mentioned in the previous section. The chapters in this book are also ordered in such a way as to help you test your knowledge about a topic after you have finished learning or revising it. In addition to chapters dedicated to the 10 individual knowledge areas, there is also a chapter dedicated to the overarching project management framework and another chapter dedicated to professional ethics - you will encounter questions related to both these topics on the exam too.

Whenever I get a chance to advise PMP candidates on how to go about studying for the PMP, I suggest them to do two readings/iterations of the primary study guides they follow. Likewise, if you are following a similar structure, after you finish reading/revising a given topic in your primary study guide (be it the PMBOK, Rita Mulcahy's PMP Exam Prep or others), try attempting all the questions in this book corresponding that topic you just studied. For example, if you finished studying the chapter on Integration Management in your primary guide, spend 30 minutes solving the 25 questions in the section for Integration Management in this book.

Preferably, use this question-bank while doing your second reading as you would probably have tested yourself using the end-of-chapter questions from your primary guide during your first reading.

The questions in this question-bank are split across individual sections as follows:

1. Project Management Framework – 20 Questions.

2. Integration Management - 25 Questions.

3. Scope Management - 25 Questions.

4. Time Management - 25 Questions.

5. Cost Management - 25 Questions.

6. Quality Management - 25 Questions.

7. Human Resources Management - 25 Questions.

8. Communications Management - 25 Questions.

9. Risk Management - 30 Questions.

10. Procurement Management - 30 Questions.

11. Stakeholder Management - 25 Questions.

12. Professional Ethics - 20 Questions.

Tip 1: While attempting questions, keep a target of completing a section in not more than 30 minutes on an average. Write down your answer choices on a piece of paper or on a notebook and only after attempting all questions in a section should you move to the solution section for that chapter to cross-check your answers.

Tip 2: If you answer less than 75-80% of the answers correctly for a given topic, revise that section from your primary study guide once more before continuing.

Note: While questions on professional ethics are generally considered easy, occasionally candidates still get these questions wrong. This is because the most obvious or 'practical' choices in real-life situations are sometimes not the most ethical choices. Go through PMI's Code of Ethics and Professional Conduct to get a good idea of what PMI states about professional ethics and conduct. You can obtain this at the following URL: https://www.pmi.org/about/ethics/code.

Project Management Framework: Questions

1. Jamie is a project manager who is working hard to complete a banking software project, but he is unable to get enough attention from his team members who are more worried about completion of process related work. Unfortunately, Jamie has no authority to assign or recruit resources. What type of organisation is Jamie likely to be working for?

    A.   Functional.

    B.   Matrix.

    C.   Expediter.

    D.   Coordinator.

2. Which of these statements regarding projects and project management is incorrect?

    A.   Project management is integrative.

    B.   Projects exist within an organisation and operate as a closed system.

C. Project processes help generate information that can be used for future projects.

D. In successful project management, the various stakeholder requirements are met.

3. In a well-managed project, the lessons-learned documentation is compiled and stored for the reference of future projects. At which stage of a project is the lessons-learned compiled?

A. At the start of the project.

B. At the end of the project.

C. Halfway through the project and at the end of the project.

D. Throughout the duration of the project.

4. Barry joined as a project manager in a functional organisation. Once he starts working on new projects, Barry is likely to find that:

A. He wields immense authority in his role and can make independent project decisions.

B. His work is easy and management systems are designed to support projects.

C. Managing projects in his organisation is difficult and management systems are not designed to support project needs efficiently.

D. He is able to easily reach out and communicate with other teams to get work done without needing to go through a functional manager.

5. A project which was estimated to use 10,000 person hours of effort ended up using 12,500 person hours of effort at

completion. What is the difference between these two figures termed?

A. Control Limit.

B. Variance.

C. Threshold Breach.

D. Project Deviation.

6. A project has many characteristics. Which of the following is not a project characteristic?

A. A project's impact ends when the project ends.

B. There might be uncertainties about the work involved in a project.

C. Some of the project deliverables may have repetitive elements.

D. A project may involve just one person.

7. Identify the incorrect statement from the choices below:

A. A project may create a capability to perform a service.

B. It is not possible to terminate projects before the deadline.

C. A project can involve a single resource.

D. A project may have multiple phases.

8. In a candid conversation with a colleague, you were told that it is sufficient to adhere to just the applicable 'standards' for a project and that 'regulations' are simply guidelines which are left to your discretion whether to follow or not. Which of the following is true?

A. Standards are guidelines established by consensus and approved by a recognised body while regulations are mandatory, government-imposed requirements.

B. Both standards and regulations are mandatory; standards are issued by the project team, while regulations are issued by the government.

C. Both standards and regulations are guidelines; standards are internal to an organisation while regulations are issued by the government.

D. Standards and regulations are synonymous terms and depending on which part of the globe you are in, any one of the two is used.

9. Brenda is a project manager who has been assigned to a large project that has been split into five phases – Analysis, Design, Implementation, Testing and Rollout. Brenda wants to use the PMBOK process groups with these separate phases. What should be the recommended approach for Brenda to follow?

A. Rename each phase with one of the process group names after discarding the original phase structure.

B. Use only some of the process groups since all of them don't apply to a large project.

C. Assign one process group to each phase.

D. Repeat all the five process groups for each phase.

10. You are managing a project to upgrade the intranet system of a travel solutions company. However, you are finding it difficult to align resources and to get tasks completed on time because the budget for your project is controlled by the infrastructure manager. What type of organisation are you working in?

A. Balanced Matrix.

B. Functional.

C. Strong Matrix.

D. Projectized.

11. Despite being a project manager in your organization, you have little authority over the projects you manage, and you are always engaged in project coordination activities. While you have a team, the team members report to their own functional managers and you, in turn, report to the PMO manager. What kind of organisation are you working in?

A. Strong Matrix.

B. Balanced Matrix.

C. Weak Matrix.

D. Functional.

12. If working in a projectized organisation, the project team:

A. Has more than one reporting manager.

B. Is unlikely to have loyalty towards the project.

C. Reports to the functional manager throughout the project.

D. Would not have a functional department to return to after the project.

13. Which of the following should a project manager study if he is keenly interested in the collection, integration and distribution of all the outputs obtained from all project management processes?

A. Work breakdown Structure (WBS).

B. Scope Management Plan.

C. Communications management Plan.

D. Project management information systems (PMIS).

14. A project manager unexpectedly quit the organisation Damien works for and now Damien is burdened with the responsibility of a new project in addition to his existing one. While still struggling to come to terms with the additional work to be done on the new project, Damien hears about another project, completed in his company the previous year, which is similar to this new project. What should Damien do?

A. Reach out to the project manager of the completed project for help.

B. Contact the project management office (PMO) and obtain historical records and guidance.

C. Wait for some more time to see if he is able to manage the work on his own.

D. Check and ensure the scope of the new project is agreed to by all the stakeholders.

15. A project manager has received a management directive that customer orders should be treated as projects and that project managers should update daily orders, resolve issues and follow up with customers to ensure all customers provide acceptance of any orders within 7 days. Each order from a customer would be worth between $50 and $5,000. Project managers need not do any planning activities and the only documentation activity they would need to carry out is to provide the daily status report. What does this situation imply?

A. The activity described is program management because there are various projects involved.

B. Since each order is a temporary endeavour, this is a project.

C. This is an operations activity as this is a recurring process.

D. Only the orders incurring revenue over $5,000 would qualify as projects and require project management.

16. The Carbon Corporation is a company in which both the functional managers and the project managers equally share responsibility in assigning priorities and directing the work of people allocated to projects. The Carbon Corporation is an example of what type of organization?

A. Traditional.

B. Matrix.

C. Functional.

D. Flat Hierarchy.

17. Carla is a solution architect who has been roped in to work on 4 different projects. However, she is finding it difficult to toggle her time between these projects and wants to know the priorities between projects. Who should Carla approach to determine priorities between projects?

A. The project managers of the individual projects.

B. The project management teams of the individual projects.

C. The project management office (PMO).

D. Carla's functional manager.

18. How would you define a program?

A. It is an internal initiative set up by an organisation's management.

B. It is a means to gain benefits and control of related projects.

C. It is a government regulated project.

D. It is a group of unrelated projects managed in a coordinated way.

19. Adam is a new project manager who has been assigned to a project that has a planned duration of 6 months. He thought it would be wise to incorporate the learning from previous projects and found an older project that was similar in nature and was completed in 18 months. He then proceeded to incorporate all the tools, techniques and checklists, without any modifications, from the old project into his current one. Which of the following statements is the most appropriate to describe Adam's action?

A. This is a perfect example of correctly reusing documents and artefacts from prior projects.

B. Adam committed a grave error of violating intellectual copyrights of the organisation's prior customer.

C. Adam followed an incorrect procedure because a project manager is supposed to create processes and documents afresh for any new projects.

D. Adam's action may have been unnecessary. What is appropriate for the project should ideally have been decided by the project team.

20. You are managing a project in which you have been contracted to deliver a complex software system to your client.

15

Your client is being billed on Time and Materials. One of your team members discovers an innovative way of coding a component and this breakthrough will potentially result in cost savings for the project and may even result in the project getting delivered two weeks ahead of schedule. What is the action you should take following this discovery?

A. This discovery should be treated as confidential information internal to your organisation and therefore need not be shared with the customer. The savings will result in additional profits for your organisation.

B. You will need to communicate this information and the current status to the customer and inform the customer that you will use the savings in cost and time to incorporate some new features.

C. You will need to communicate this information and the current status to the customer and inform them of the potential changes to cost and schedule.

D. You should communicate the savings in cost and time to the customer and also notify your billing department that they need to prepare an additional invoice to the customer for 50% of the cost being saved.

Project Management Framework: Solutions

1. Answer A. A project manager receives the least support for a project and has practically no authority to assign resources in a functional organization. The last two choices are not organisation types.

2. Answer B. Projects cannot operate as a closed system though they exist within an organisation. Projects take input data from the organization and also deliver back capabilities to the organisation. All other statements are correct.

3. Answer D. Lessons learned documentation is a part of an organisation's Organisational Process Assets (OPA) and this is compiled and stored throughout the duration of the project.

4. Answer C. In a functional organisation, such as the one Barry has joined, projects will typically lack management systems to support their needs. This would make it difficult for a project manager to run a project efficiently. Communication with team members in such organisations will also be typically cascaded via a functional manager and the return communication happens in a similar manner too.

5. Answer B. The correct term is 'Variance' – this is defined as a quantifiable deviation, departure, or divergence, from a known baseline of expected value.

6. Answer A. A project's impact may far outlast the project itself (think of a unique product or service created in a project that will be in use for a much longer period after project completion). All other choices are valid project characteristics. It is possible that a project may involve only one person, a single organisational unit, or multiple organisational units. Certain project deliverables may have repetitive elements. Lastly, because of the unique nature of the work involved in a project, there will be uncertainties (these are often captured as project risks).

7. Answer B. It is possible to terminate any project before its deadline if it no longer meets the requirement of the performing organisation. All other statements are correct.

8. Answer A. Standards are guidelines developed by a recognized body and are established by consensus. On the other hand, regulations are mandatory government-imposed requirements.

9. Answer D. Process groups and project phases are different - each project phase should contain all the process groups.

10. Answer B. It is only in Functional and Weak Matrix Organizations that the functional manager (in this case, the infrastructure manager) controls the budget.

11. Answer C. Since the team members report to functional managers, it is evident that the organisation can only be following a weak matrix structure or a functional structure. The presence of the PMO indicates the organization is not strictly functional and therefore it is a weak matrix organisation. A project manager's role in a weak matrix organization is that of a project coordinator or expeditor. Contrarily, a project manager has high authority and complete control in a Projectized organization. In a Balanced Matrix Organization, though the project manager does not have absolute control, the organization still recognizes the need to have a dedicated project manager and therefore he/she is on an even footing with functional managers.

12. Answer D. The primary disadvantage of a projectized organization is that once the project team is dispersed after the completion of the project, they do not have a functional department (home) to return to.

13. Answer D. The scope management plan and the WBS focus only on the project scope while the communications management plan addresses the various aspects of communication in the project. The only choice that deals with the collection, integration and distribution of information is the PMIS.

14. Answer B. A project manager can do many things in a situation such as this. However, asking the previous manager for help might not be the best idea because the other project manager may not have time to spare or may not be experienced at mentoring. Waiting to see if the work can be managed in due time is not advisable as this is a reactive measure, and project managers are expected to act pro-actively. Getting an agreement on the scope from various stakeholders is unlikely to help Damien in this situation. By contacting the PMO, Damien would gain access to the knowledge of prior projects and historical records; the PMO team is also designated to help project managers in similar situations, and therefore, option B, is the best option.

15. Answer C. Despite the use of the word 'projects' the situation described is clearly a recurring process. This is therefore an operations activity and not a project or a program. Also, there is no data to suggest that the last option is true.

16. Answer B. It is only in a Matrix organization that the project manager shares responsibility with the functional manager for assigning priorities and directing the work of people allocated to projects. All other options are invalid.

17. Answer C. The question is about priorities between projects. Project managers, project teams and functional managers cannot determine priorities between projects and this is the function of the PMO (project management organisation).

18. Answer B. Programs are a means to gain benefits and controls of related projects. All other options are incorrect. The last option is wrong because it states 'unrelated' instead of 'related'.

19. Answer D. The right response here is that Adam's action may have been unnecessary. The differences in the durations of the earlier project and Adam's project suggest that it is unlikely that the current project can have exactly the same processes applied and some amount of modifications might be required. Remaining responses are invalid. Adam is unlikely to have infringed intellectual copyrights of the prior customer since organisations have clear guidelines on what information can be included in the Organisational Process Assets (and any copyrighted information will be excluded).

20. Answer C. The project manager should communicate accurate information on the project status. Subsequently, he could get into discussions with the customer on how to utilise the cost savings – this activity, however, needs to be carried out following the appropriate procedure.

Knowledge Area 1 – Integration Management: Questions

1. You have been appointed as the new Director of Customer Delivery in an organisation. There are ten projects that are in various stages of delivery by the department and you would like to know the business justification for each of these projects. Which of the following documents should you review for each project to understand this?

    A.   The Project Management Plan.

    B.   The Delivery Plan.

    C.   The Project Charter.

    D.   The Scope Management Plan.

2. Bernie is a project manager in an Information Technology company. For one of the projects he is currently managing, he receives a request from a stakeholder to make a major change that would cost additional money and push the delivery timelines forward. Bernie got the change request approved after following the necessary process and he has to now

incorporate this change into his project. What should he do next?

- A. He needs to ensure that he tracks this change against the project's baseline so that he knows how much it eventually costs.

- B. He needs to modify the Project Charter to include this change.

- C. He needs to incorporate the change into the project baseline so that he can track the project properly.

- D. He needs to use the Project Management Information System to ensure that the work is performed.

3. While running a telecommunications project, you come to know of a critical problem that threatens to delay your project, which in turn is also very likely to impact the business of the stakeholders. The full impact of the problem is yet to be determined and it will take a day to completely assess the problem. What is the best course of action in the given situation?

- A. Update the findings in the lessons learned and add it to the organisation's OPA.

- B. Setup an emergency meeting with the stakeholders and inform them of the situation and that you will need one more day to provide complete information of the problem.

- C. Initiate a change request and submit this to the Change Control Board at the earliest.

- D. Go through the project charter to check who is authorised to make decisions.

4. A stakeholder from a project you are managing has just raised a change request. Which of the following does this imply?

    A.   The project is now in the Direct and Manage Project Work process and therefore you can go ahead and implement the requested change.

    B.   Though the project charter is complete, you cannot commence work because you have to now make a change to the scope baseline.

    C.   The change needs to now go through the approval process before it can be implemented.

    D.   Since the change is a defect, it must be repaired right away.

5. Which of the following statements about the Project Management Plan is incorrect?

    A.   It is not the document that sanctions authority to the project manager.

    B.   It does not contain the Communications Management Plan.

    C.   It contains the performance baseline.

    D.   It contains schedule baseline.

6. The project sponsor of a project you are managing cancels the project because he no longer sees any business value coming from it. What is the next thing you need to do?

    A.   Reassign people who have been working on your project to new projects.

    B.   Refuse to stop the project since it was already approved and continue with the work.

C. Check with your PMO team on how to use the rest of the budget.

D. Initiate closure procedures to close the project and update the lessons learned.

7. While managing a software project, one of your senior developers goes on indefinite leave due to a personal emergency. What's the first thing you should do in such a situation?

A. Figure out the impact of the developer's absence on the project.

B. Inform all stakeholders that the project will now be delayed indefinitely.

C. Inform team members that they will have to work overtime to make up for the resource loss.

D. Contact Human Resources to hire a replacement.

8. Jeremy is the project manager for a logistics project and he realises there are several approved changes pending implementation; he needs to decide how to apply project resources in order to implement these changes. What should he do?

A. He should reject the changes because they would delay the project.

B. He should prioritise these changes and then announce them to the team.

C. He should consult the prioritisation management plan for guidance on prioritising new changes.

D. He should call a meeting with all stakeholders to decide whether to go ahead with the changes.

9. Which of the following statements about the project charter is incorrect?

- A. The project charter grants authority to the project manager to manage the project.

- B. It is issued by the project sponsor.

- C. It provides a milestone schedule of the project.

- D. The project manager must be consulted when it is being created.

10. Jacob is a project manager who has just received a change request from a stakeholder. Jacob's instinct tells him the implementation of this change might jeopardise his project schedule. Therefore, he calls for a meeting with the project team where he announces they need to initiate change control immediately. Which of the following is not an output of the process that follows?

- A. Change Requests.

- B. Project document updates.

- C. Project Management Plan updates.

- D. Change Request status updates.

11. A project you are managing is on-track and is due for completion two days ahead of schedule. However, you have now been approached by a key stakeholder who requests an important change in the project that might require one day's effort. What should you do?

- A. Ask the stakeholder to send an email outlining the change and then make the change.

- B. Implement the change since you are already ahead of schedule.

C.   Refuse to make the change until the stakeholder documents it in a Change Request.

D.   Let the stakeholders know you are open to the change and ask them to contact the project sponsor also.

12. Dan has been asked to select between 3 new projects. Project A has a Net Present Value (NPV) of $45,000 and can be completed in 1 year, Project B has an NPV of $56,000 and can be completed in 18 months and Project C has an NPV of $100,000 and can be completed in 2 years. Which of these projects should he opt for?

A.   Project A.

B.   Project B.

C.   Project C.

D.   None. NPV is not a criteria used for project selection.

13. Which of the following is not true of a work authorisation system?

A.   It authorises the start of work packages or activities.

B.   It is part of the project management information system (PMIS).

C.   It manages when and in which sequence work is done.

D.   It determines who does which activity.

14. A newly appointed project manager has found several changes that were made to the project charter. Whose primary responsibility is it to determine whether any given change is necessary in a Project charter?

A.   The Project Manager.

B. The Program Manager.

C. The Project Team.

D. The Project Sponsor.

15. A project manager's role is often said to be that of an integrator. What does this imply?

    A. It implies that the PM has to integrate different project parts into a program.

    B. It implies that the PM makes the team work as a single unit.

    C. It implies that the PM puts all the individual pieces of the project into a cohesive whole.

    D. It implies that the PM's role is more limited in a project than that of his team members'.

16. Preparing a project charter is among the very first activities on a project, but for what purpose can the project charter be used when the project is approaching completion?

    A. To check whether a new scope change should be approved.

    B. To ensure all project documentation is complete.

    C. To determine whether the change control system is effective.

    D. To understand the business case.

17. When a project management plan is prepared, it should be done so with realistic goals and expectations. Which of the following would be the MOST appropriate way to create a project management plan?

A. The project sponsor should create the project management plan after consulting with the project manager.

B. The project manager should create the project plan after consulting with the senior management team.

C. The functional manager should create the project plan after consulting with the project manager.

D. The project manager should create the project plan after taking inputs from the project team.

18. You are a project manager who just received a change request from a customer. The change seems easy to complete and will not affect the current project schedule. What should you do NEXT?

A. Implement the change as soon as possible.

B. Evaluate any potential impacts of the change on other project constraints.

C. Take the change to the Change Control Board.

D. Get the project sponsor's approval.

19. A project has just moved to the Close Project or Phase process after the completion of all technical work. Choose the activity that still needs to be carried out:

A. Plan Risk responses.

B. Validate Scope.

C. Complete Lessons Learnt.

D. Verify the output of Direct and Manage Project Work.

20. You are a project manager who has created a new Project Management Plan. However, just before you baseline it, a stakeholder detects a key omission and requests you to modify the project management plan to accommodate this. What should you do?

    A.   Ask the stakeholder to submit a change request.

    B.   Consult with the Change Control Board.

    C.   Reject the request from the stakeholder after informing him what he requested is a scope creep.

    D.   Make the requested change in the Project Management Plan.

21. Deborah, a project manager in Carlson IT Corporation, has submitted her resignation. Chris is the new project manager who has been appointed as Deborah's replacement. What should be the first thing that Chris should do when he takes over as the new project manager?

    A.   Determine a management strategy.

    B.   Inform team members of his objectives.

    C.   Check cost and schedule performance.

    D.   Check the status of various risks.

22. The Change Control System and the Configuration Management System are both integral to project management. What is the difference between the two?

    A.   Both are part of Environment Enterprise Factors.

    B.   The Change control system is part of the PMIS while the Configuration Management System is not.

C. The Configuration Management System is part of the PMIS while the Change Control System is not.

D. The Change Control System mainly deals with the changes to the project baseline while the Configuration Management System mainly deals with changes in product specifications.

23. Which of the following statements is NOT true regarding an approved change request?

A. It is an output of Direct and Manage Project Work process.

B. It is scheduled and implemented by the project team.

C. It may result in changes to the cost baseline.

D. It may result in changes to the schedule baseline.

24. You are working on a CRM project and the operations team discovers an issue with the existing CRM that needs to be addressed via a change. The management team raises a change request to the Change Control Board to include this change as part of your on-going project. However, when you analyse the change, you reach a conclusion that the new change does not fit within the project charter for your existing project. Instead it has to be incorporated concurrently and with a different set of resources. What would be the best thing to do in this case?

A. Revise the project schedule with inputs from the operations team.

B. Get help from stakeholders to validate the scope of the new work.

C. Develop a new project charter.

D. Try to identify specific changes to the existing project work.

25. A project manager has to choose the most profitable among four projects. He finds that Project A has an internal rate of return (IRR) of 20%, Project B has an IRR of 25%, Project C has an IRR of 36% and Project D has an IRR of 28%. Which project should he choose?

    A.   Project A.

    B.   Project B.

    C.   Project C.

    D.   Project D.

Knowledge Area 1 – Integration Management: Solutions

1. Answer C. The Project charter is the document that provides the details of the business justification for any given project.

2. Answer C. The first thing that needs to be done after a change has been approved is to update the project baseline. This will ensure the project is correctly tracked against the new baseline.

3. Answer B. The best course of action in this situation is to provide clear communication to the stakeholders of the problem at first. A change request is not a logical option here given that assessment of the problem isn't complete. Updating lessons learned isn't the best course of action at this time and consulting the project charter isn't relevant to the situation in hand.

4. Answer C. Change requests are accepted as an input in the Perform Integrated Change Control process only and the next step after receiving a change is to get it approved. None of the other options is correct.

5. Answer B. All the individual management plans including the Communications Management Plan are part of the Project Management Plan.

6. Answer D. A project can be cancelled midway for several reasons. However, once a project has been cancelled, the next thing to do is to follow process and initiate the formal closure of the project.

7. Answer A. When a resource is no longer available, the project manager has to figure out how to move forward next. And the first step is to estimate and quantify what would the impact be of the absence and then decide how to proceed.

8. Answer B. The priority of the changes must be determined by the project manager. Since the changes have already been approved (ie. they went through the Change Control Board) they cannot be rejected. Also, there is no such plan called a prioritisation management plan and lastly, calling all the stakeholders for consensus would be unnecessary since these changes were approved.

9. Answer D. Though the Project Manager may be consulted when a project charter is created, this is not mandatory. In many instances, the project manager may not even be aware of the project charter at the time of its creation.

10. Answer A. While this question has a lot of extraneous information, the question simply asks which option provided is not an output of the 'Perform Integrated Change Control' process. Change Requests are an input to the mentioned process, while all the others are outputs.

11. Answer C. Any new change needs to go through the Perform Integrated Change Control process and for this each change request needs to be documented. A new change cannot be taken up until it is formally documented and submitted to the Perform Integrated Change Process.

12. Answer C. Dan should select project C because it has the highest NPV. NPV already considers timeframe during calculation and therefore the information provided on the number of years for completion is irrelevant. Last option is incorrect because NPV is a valid economic model used for project selection.

13. Answer D. The work authorisation system does not determine who does which activity (this is the function of the responsibility assignment matrix). All the other statements are true.

14. Answer D. The Project Sponsor issues the project charter and is primarily responsible for determining whether any changes are necessary in a project charter.

15. Answer C. A project manager integrates (or puts together) various activities of a project into a cohesive whole. This is what the statement implies.

16. Answer A. If a new change request is raised late in the project, one way to determine whether it should be approved is by determining whether the change comes within the purview of the project charter. If not, it should be rejected, moved to another project, or initiated as a separate project of its own. With respect to Option D, a project charter is used to understand the business case but this is done at the time of the commencement of the project and not when the project is approaching closure. Options B and C are incorrect statements.

17. Answer D. This question indirectly asks who creates the Project Management Plan. It is the project manager who creates this after taking inputs from the project team. While it might help by taking inputs from the senior management team, the inputs of the actual team that works on the project is far more valuable in creating a realistic plan as it is the team that can properly gauge the amount of actual work to be done and the time required.

18. Answer B. While the proposed change has no impact on schedule, there is no information provided about its impact on the other project constraints. Therefore, the next thing to do would be to evaluate any impacts on scope, cost, quality, risk and resources also before submitting this change to the Change Control Board.

19. Answer C. Completing the Lessons Learnt is the only activity that belongs to the Close Project or Phase process. All the other activities belong to processes that are part of prior process groups and hence these would have already been completed in the project at this stage.

20. Answer D. Since the Project Management Plan is yet to be baselined, this omission can be included in the Project Management Plan without having to approach the CCB, without asking the stakeholder to raise a change request, and without needing to treat this as a scope creep.

21. Answer A. Before doing anything else, Chris needs to know what he is going to do and for that he needs to develop a management strategy. Doing so will provide him a framework for the remaining choices presented and any other activities that need to be carried out.

22. Answer D. The option A does not show a difference while options B and C are incorrect – both the Change Control System and the Configuration Management System are a part of an organisation's PMIS. The difference between the two systems in simple words is that the Change Control System mainly deals with the changes to the project baseline while the Configuration Management System mainly deals with changes in product specifications.

23. Answer A. Approved Change requests are INPUTS to the Direct and Manage Work Process and are not outputs of this process.

24. Answer C. Since this change doesn't come under the purview of the existing project charter and is a separate unit of work that requires a different set of resources, the best course of action would be to initiate this as a separate project and for this a new project charter needs to be created. All the other options try to tackle the problem as a part of/addition to the existing project itself.

25. Answer C. The greater the internal rate of return, the more profitable the project and hence, the best option is Project C with 36%.

Knowledge Area 2 – Scope Management: Questions

1. You are the project manager in-charge of delivering a new payroll system to your client organisation. When the project is in the execution phase, a stakeholder raises a concern that a requirement he had asked for has not been included in the deliverables. Which document should the project manager refer in order to check the approved list of deliverables?

    A.   Risk Management Plan.

    B.   Project Charter.

    C.   Project Scope Statement.

    D.   Scope Management Plan.

2. Which of the following statements about the WBS is NOT true?

    A.   It is a part of the scope baseline.

    B.   It includes only deliverables required for the project.

C. It is broken down further into smaller work packages.

D. It is an activity.

3. Which are the three components that comprise the scope baseline?

A. Scope Statement, WBS, and WBS dictionary.

B. Project management plan, WBS, and Scope Statement.

C. Project management plan, scope management plan, and WBS dictionary.

D. Risk management plan, scope management plan, and Scope Statement.

4. At the time of delivery, a stakeholder has raised a complaint that one of his initial requirements was not fulfilled. What should the project manager refer to know the corresponding deliverable for each approved requirement?

A. Project management plan.

B. Scope Statement.

C. Requirements Traceability Matrix.

D. WBS.

5. A project manager needs inputs on how a certain customer requirement can be taken forward and for this he needs inputs from six key stakeholders. The project manager knows from experience that if he were to get these six stakeholders in an open group discussion, it would typically lead to an open conflict between them. Therefore, he sends a request for information to each of these stakeholders and captures their responses anonymously. The project manager then compiles all their individual responses and then sends the results back to these stakeholders for further review to reach an agreement.

What type of group-decision making technique did this project manager use?

   A.   Benchmarking.

   B.   Plurality.

   C.   Unanimity.

   D.   Delphi-Technique.

6. A new software developer has joined your project and he wants a detailed description of the work that needs to be done on the project. Which of the following documents is LEAST likely to help him?

   A.   Project Scope Statement.

   B.   WBS.

   C.   Project Statement of Work.

   D.   Requirements Traceability Matrix.

7. Your project team is working on a complex project involving some technology they have not worked on before. They realise that in order to execute the project successfully, they will need to organise and group requirements in the most efficient means possible. Which of the following techniques would be the most useful for them?

   A.   Delphi Technique.

   B.   Brainstorming.

   C.   Affinity Diagrams.

   D.   Nominal group technique.

8. The project you are managing is 50% complete and at this stage is due for a review by senior management. During a review such as this one, a variance analysis is usually conducted. What is the purpose of a variance analysis?

- A. It is used to evaluate any cost variances on the project.

- B. It is used to measure the deviation from the project management plan.

- C. It is used to measure the project variances against the scope baseline.

- D. It is used to measure schedule variances on the project.

9. Which of the following provides a way to manage and control costs, schedule and scope at a level above the work package?

- A. Cost breakdown package.

- B. Control account.

- C. Work account.

- D. Component level.

10. What does decomposition mean in the context of the Scope Management processes?

- A. The breaking down of customer requirements into manageable units.

- B. The breaking down of work to the level of work packages.

- C. The breaking down of work to lowest levels of detail.

D. The breaking down of the project scope to manageable bits.

11. A project team has just completed some work and submitted it to the customer for verification. The team will commence the planning for the next phase once the customer finishes verification. The work product is found satisfactory by the customer who acknowledges that it meets the project requirement. What is this work product now called?

A. An accepted deliverable that requires further approval from the project sponsor.

B. An accepted deliverable that is an output of the control scope process.

C. An accepted deliverable that requires a formal sign off from the customer.

D. None of the above.

12. The work breakdown structure (WBS) often uses a hierarchical (or an alternate) numbering system. This helps the project team to:

A. Use the WBS in the PMIS.

B. Estimate costs for elements.

C. Easily identify the elements in various levels.

D. Help justify project costs.

13. Identify the key output of the Validate Scope process from the following.

A. Updated schedule estimates.

B. Updates to the PMIS.

C. Updates to the scope management plan.

D. Accepted project deliverables.

14. You are a project manager who is managing a telecommunications project. One of the new hires in your team comes to you asking for complete details of the work package he is supposed to deliver. Which of the following documents would have the details the team member is seeking?

A. WBS dictionary.

B. Activity List.

C. Project Scope Statement.

D. Requirement Traceability matrix.

15. Dmitry is running a 1-year project that is on track for completion within scheduled time and within budget. Nevertheless, a month before completion, he gets to know the stakeholders are dissatisfied with the deliverables and this situation is now likely to add a month's delay to the project. Which of the following processes could have prevented the situation Dmitry is now facing?

A. Control Scope.

B. Define Scope.

C. Control Schedule.

D. Monitor and Control Risks.

16. Before preparing the weekly project report that he needs to submit to stakeholders, a project manager goes around asking team members what amount of their work is complete. An experienced team member, who has a reputation for being difficult to manage, retaliates asking "Completion status of what work?" when asked how much of his work was complete.

The project manager, exasperated with the team-member's behaviour, complains to the team member's boss about his lack of co-operation. However, which of the following is MOST likely to be the real problem here?

A. The project manager does not have authority over the team-member.

B. Work packages were not assigned by the project manager.

C. There is no adequate reward system in place to motivate the team members.

D. The team member lacks the skill to carry out his work.

17. Who is responsible for the development of the scope baseline? Choose the BEST option from the below:

A. The project sponsor.

B. The project manager

C. All stakeholders.

D. The project team.

18. At what stage of a project should the Validate Scope process be carried out?

A. At the beginning of the project.

B. At the very end of the project.

C. At the end of every phase of the project.

D. During the planning phase of the project.

19. A project manager who has been newly assigned to a project receives a request from a stakeholder to add new scope

to the project. After going through some of the older correspondence emails, the project manager gets to know this same request had been raised earlier when the project charter was being prepared and the project sponsor had declined to fund this request and therefore it was not included in the project scope at that time. What should the project manager do in this situation?

A. Inform the stakeholder the scope cannot be added.

B. Go back to the project sponsor and inform him/her about the request.

C. Check the project schedule and accommodate it in the scope if there is no impact on the schedule.

D. Evaluate the scope impact.

20. A new project manager is struggling to manage his project when the project scope is being progressively elaborated. His more experienced PMP certified colleague advises him that tools such as the WBS could immensely help him at this point. Which of the following statements regarding the WBS is true?

A. It defines the business justification for the project.

B. It can be used for communicating with the customer.

C. It shows high-level details of the various project risks.

D. It shows the dates against each work package.

21. A project stakeholder initiates a change request that gets submitted to the Change Control Board (CCB). After careful consideration of the various impacts of the submitted change, the CCB rejects the change. What should be the BEST course of action for the project manager?

A. He should resubmit it to the CCB as the change is important to the stakeholder.

B. He should ask the justification for the rejection from the CCB.

C. He should document the outcome of the change request.

D. He should inform his project sponsor to force CCB to reconsider the request.

22. Which of the below processes is the Validate Scope process closely related to?

A. Control Costs.

B. Perform Quality Assurance.

C. Control Quality.

D. Control Schedule.

23. A software project is running 6 days ahead of schedule and is within budget. It is currently in the development phase which is almost complete. This will be followed by the testing and implementation phases. Which of the below processes should the project manager be MOST concerned about before the project moves into the final phase?

A. Control Costs.

B. Control Schedule.

C. Control Quality.

D. Validate Scope.

24. Decomposition is a process that is carried out to ensure the work on a project gets managed efficiently. Which of the following statements does NOT state how to decompose work?

A. It should be done till the work can be carried out by just one person.

B. It should be done till it reaches the level of work packages.

C. It should be done till the level at which it can be realistically estimated.

D. It can be done till the level at which work can be outsourced or contracted out.

25. What is the primary purpose of capturing a user story?

A. To document past issues from previous projects.

B. To document product functionalities or features required by the customer

C. To avoid further communication during requirement gathering.

D. To expedite the requirement gathering process.

Knowledge Area 2 – Scope Management: Solutions

1. Answer C. The Project Scope Statement captures the list of agreed deliverables (and also what is not part of the project).

2. Answer D. The WBS is not an activity, but rather, the work products or deliverables that result from an activity or many activities. The PMBOK defines the work breakdown structure as a "deliverable oriented hierarchical decomposition of the work to be executed by the project team."

3. Answer A. The Scope Statement, WBS and WBS dictionary are the three constituents of the scope baseline.

4. Answer C. The Requirements Traceability Matrix maps each feature and element of a deliverable back to the original requirement raised. Therefore, to see which deliverable fulfils a given requirement, the project manager needs to refer this document.

5. Answer D. The Delphi-technique is used to avoid head-on confrontations and in this method of group-decision making, views are gathered anonymously.

6. Answer C. The Project Statement of Work is a preliminary high-level document that is an input to the project charter (in the initiating phase) and has the least level of detail in comparison with the other documents. All the other documents are prepared during the planning phase and contain far more details.

7. Answer C. In Affinity diagrams, ideas and requirements are grouped and organised on similarities and therefore is the most useful in this situation.

8. Answer C. Variance analysis is used to specifically measure the project variances against the scope baseline.

9. Answer B. A control account helps aggregate and analyse work performance data regarding cost, schedule and scope and is a way to manage and control costs, schedule and scope at a level above the work package.

10. Answer B. Decomposition is the process via which work is broken down till the level of work packages.

11. Answer C. This work product is now an acceptable deliverable which requires a formal sign-off from the customer.

12. Answer C. Using a numbering system helps project team members to easily determine the level in the WBS where a given element is found. Additionally, it also helps locate details of this element in the WBS dictionary.

13. Answer D. The output of the Validate Scope process is the customer acceptance of the project deliverables. The updates mentioned in the remaining options take place during the planning phase.

14. Answer A. The WBS dictionary defines each element in the WBS and also provides detailed descriptions of the work packages in the WBS. None of the other documents provide a detailed description of the work packages - which is what the team member needs.

15. Answer B. This question asks which process could have 'prevented' the situation. Therefore, options A, C and D are incorrect – they are all from the Monitoring and Controlling process group and can only address a problem and not prevent it. The situation described could have been prevented by proper planning and by clearly defining the project deliverables in the 'Define Scope' process which is part of the planning phase.

16. Answer B. The problem in this scenario can be understood from the team-member's question which indicates he does not seem to know what work he was supposed to do. If there was a clear WBS and if work packages had been correctly assigned to team members, then this team member would have had clarity on what his work was. The description of him being difficult is simply meant to distract one from the actual problem. There is no evidence to suggest that the project manager lacks authority or that the team member lacks skill. While reward systems will help motivate the team, the problem here is not a lack of motivation, but a lack of understanding on what the team-member's work is.

17. Answer D. The project team is responsible for the development of the scope baseline (which includes the WBS, WBS dictionary and project scope statement) after taking inputs from all the stakeholders.

18. Answer C. The Validate Scope process is part of Monitoring and Controlling and should be carried out at the end of every phase of the project to get sign-off from the customer for the deliverables completed in that phase.

19. Answer A. Since this same request was previously evaluated and rejected by the sponsor, the stakeholder needs to be informed the scope cannot be added. There is no point in further evaluation or in going back to the sponsor again for the same request since it was already considered and rejected once.

20. Answer B. The WBS does not show dates against work packages, it does not provide business justification (this is provided in the project charter) and it doesn't provide details of project risks (this is captured in the risk register). However, the WBS could be used as an effective communication tool, at the time of progressive elaboration, to communicate with stakeholders and to let them understand the project scope.

21. Answer C. The details and outcome of change request should be documented so that in future if this change is raised again, this documentation will serve as an ideal reference. It would not serve any purpose resubmitting the change since it was already evaluated before being rejected. At the time of rejection the CCB would've clearly outlined the reasons for rejection and hence asking for justification is unnecessary. Trying to use the sponsor to bypass the board's authority or influence is considered unethical and shouldn't be considered.

22. Answer C. The Validate Scope process is closely related to the Control Quality process. While Control quality is used to check the correctness of a deliverable, Validate Scope is used to check for acceptance of a deliverable.

23. Answer D. Without the acceptance of the customer, the project will not be able to move to the next phase. Validate Scope is the process where customer acceptance is obtained and therefore it is the process the project manager should be most concerned about.

24. Answer A. The lowest level of decomposition is the work package level and hence, statement B is true. Statements C and D are both characteristics of a work package and therefore true. However, a work package may be worked upon by more than one person depending on the activities that emanate from it and therefore statement A is false.

25. Answer B. User stories are often captured during facilitated workshops and the main purpose of capturing a user story is to document product functionalities or features as envisioned by the customer.

Knowledge Area 3 – Time Management: Questions

1. Which of the following is a network diagram NOT used for?

    A.   To justify the time estimate for a project.

    B.   To show project progress.

    C.   To show the interdependency between various activities.

    D.   To show associated costs of interlinked activities.

2. Which of the following is the MOST appropriate description of what a critical path is?

    A.   It is the shortest path through the network.

    B.   It is the shortest path that can no longer be compressed in the network.

    C.   It is the longest path through the network.

D. It is the longest path through the network that contains zero float.

3. Estimating activity resources and activity duration are crucial processes in schedule management. Which of the following statements regarding estimations is NOT true?

A. Estimations are more accurate if smaller-sized work components are estimated.

B. Padding is an unaccepted practice while making estimations.

C. Time and Cost estimates are not interrelated.

D. Historical information (part of OPA) can be very useful in improving estimates.

4. For a new project, a project manager employs a technique in which he uses expert judgement and refers historical records of previous projects to reach an estimate for that project. What kind of estimating technique did he use?

A. Three-Point Estimating.

B. Analogous Estimating.

C. Parametric Estimating.

D. PERT technique.

5. A project manager is in the planning stage of a project and realises he may not be able to plan to the lowest level of detail because some components are still unknown. Therefore, he decides to plan the work a level higher, wait for the project to commence, and then plan the lowest level of work, once further details are available. What kind of planning practice has this project manager employed?

A. Rolling Wave Planning.

B.   Continuous Planning.

C.   Flexible Planning.

D.   Sequential Planning.

6. As part of an on-going software implementation project, the project team must setup a new testing environment before they can commence the software testing. This is an example of:

A.   Discretionary dependency.

B.   Mandatory dependency.

C.   External dependency.

D.   Internal dependency.

7. You are trying to determine the time it would take for your upcoming software project to complete and eventually determine that it was most likely to complete in 35 weeks. However, if the additional resources you had asked for get allocated to the project, you believe that you can complete the project in as early as 30 weeks. On the flip side, if the hardware consignment gets delayed, the project might take up to 45 weeks. Using the 3-point estimate (P.E.R.T method), what would be the likely completion timeline for the project?

A.   30 Weeks.

B.   33 Weeks.

C.   40.5 Weeks.

D.   35.8 Weeks.

8. A project manager and his project team are planning the work to be done on a project. They have reviewed the customer requirements and have created an outline of the work breakdown structure and its corresponding WBS

dictionary. They are now breaking down the work packages into smaller increments. What are they now trying to create?

A.   A scope elaboration list.

B.   A deliverable list.

C.   An activity list.

D.   A milestone list.

9. In a recent management review, it was decided the project you are currently running has to be finished 2 weeks ahead of the planned schedule. Accordingly, you have been requested to fast-track your project. Which of the following correctly states a disadvantage and an advantage associated with fast tracking?

A.   It could increase costs but it allows some activities to be run in parallel.

B.   It could increase risks but it allows some activities to be run in parallel.

C.   It could increase costs but it allows activities to be run overtime.

D.   It could cause team burnout but it re-uses resources.

10. A project manager has identified the various activities to be done on his project and has marked these activities in the following grid. Identify the path with zero float from the details provided.

Activity	Preceding Activity	Duration (weeks)
Start	None	0
A	Start	3
B	A	4
C	A	6
D	B,C	10
E	C	10
F	D,E	5
G	E	9
End	F,G	0

A. Path Start-A-B-D-F-End.

B. Path Start-A-C-D-F-End.

C. Path Start-A-C-E-G-End.

D. Path Start-A-C-E-F-End.

11. For the project mentioned in the previous question, the customer has requested the Activity F to be cut by 2 weeks. What will be the impact on the project schedule, when this is carried out?

A. There will be no change in overall project schedule.

B. The project schedule will decrease by 2 weeks.

C. The project will finish earlier if Activity B is also cut by 1 week.

D. The project will finish earlier if Activity D is also cut by 1 week.

12. For the same project mentioned in the penultimate question, the customer has demanded to reduce the project schedule by 2 weeks. As far as the existing project schedule is concerned, what does this imply?

   A. The project would no longer be deliverable since the project cannot be cut by two weeks.

   B. The project now has a negative float.

   C. The project manager will need to fast track the project.

   D. The project manager will need to crash the project.

13. You are assigned a project with the following activities: Activity A can start as soon as the project starts and will take 20 days. Activity B can also start once the project starts and will take 25 days. Activity C can start only after Activity A is complete and will take 50 days. Activity D can start only after activities B and C are complete, and will take 30 days. Activity E can commence only after activity C completes and will take 12 days. Activity F can commence only after activity E completes and will take 20 days. Activities F and D are the last activities in the project. Which of the below statements is TRUE if the activity B takes 10 extra days?

   A. The critical path becomes 65 days.

   B. The new critical path is Start-B-D-End.

   C. The critical path increases by 10 days.

   D. The critical path remains Start-A-C-E-F-End.

14. Dominic is a project manager who has just taken over a project from Phil, who is leaving their company. The project was still in the planning phase when Dominic took over and he now wants to check what Phil had planned for managing

schedule changes. Which of the following would be BEST suited for this purpose?

A.   Staff management plan.

B.   Communications management plan.

C.   Schedule management plan.

D.   Generic management plan.

15. Project manager Dominic, with assistance from his project team, has prepared the WBS, the WBS dictionary, the estimates for each work package and also the network diagram. What should he do NEXT?

A.   Validate scope.

B.   Sequence the activities.

C.   Create a preliminary schedule.

D.   Complete risk management.

16. A project activity has an early start (ES) of day 2, a late start (LS) of day 11, an early finish (EF) of day 7, and a late finish (LF) of day 16. This indicates that this activity is:

A.   Having a lag.

B.   On the critical path.

C.   Not on the critical path.

D.   Progressing as per schedule.

17. In your latest project review, it was identified that your project is likely to complete only 4 days after the desired completion date. There are no additional resources available for allocation. Your project has a benefit cost ratio of 1.3, has

low risk and its various activities have discretionary dependencies. Given these details, which of the following is the BEST course of action to complete the project on time?

   A.   Remove an activity from the project.

   B.   Reduce the number of resources.

   C.   Make more activities in parallel.

   D.   Crash the project.

18. You have just made some changes to your project to ensure you use a constant number of resources every month. What have you just carried out?

   A.   Crashing.

   B.   Fast-tracking.

   C.   Resource levelling.

   D.   Buffering.

19. Which of the following is a benefit of the analogous estimating technique?

   A.   It is among the most accurate estimation techniques.

   B.   It gives a clear indication to the project manager whether the project schedule is achievable.

   C.   It is based on a detailed understanding of the work requirements.

   D.   It aligns the project team with the management team's expectations.

20. Both milestone charts and bar charts are used for project planning and reporting. But when are milestone charts used instead of bar charts?

    A.   When analysing risks.

    B.   When reporting to team members.

    C.   When reporting to the management.

    D.   When used in the planning phase.

21. A project you are managing has multiple critical paths. Which of the following statements is the BEST description of how this will impact the project?

    A.   The project becomes easier to manage.

    B.   The project becomes more expensive.

    C.   The project risk increases.

    D.   Additional resources will be required.

22. Peter is a project manager who has been instructed to complete his project one week ahead of the originally planned schedule. Therefore, he is now looking at the cost associated with crashing some of the project activities. The BEST approach to crashing project activities will also take into account:

    A.   The client's opinion on which activities to crash.

    B.   The sponsor's opinion on which activities to crash and in which order.

    C.   Peter's manager's opinion on which activities to crash.

    D.   Risk impact of crashing each project activity.

23. What is the standard deviation of an activity that has an optimistic estimate of 14 days and a pessimistic estimate of 20 days?

    A.   1

    B.   1.5

    C.   2

    D.   1.2

24. Which of the following is a key output of the Control Schedule process?

    A.   Change Requests.

    B.   Updates to Enterprise Environment Factors.

    C.   Updates to the Risk Register.

    D.   Work performance information.

25. Project managers employ the use of heuristics when managing projects. What is a heuristic?

    A.   It is a scheduling technique.

    B.   It is a tool used for planning.

    C.   It is a tool used during monitoring and controlling.

    D.   It is a commonly accepted rule.

Knowledge Area 3 – Time Management: Solutions

1. Answer D. A project network diagram is used to justify project schedule estimates, show the dependencies between various activities and can also be used to report project progress. However, it does not show associated costs for these interlinked activities.

2. Answer D. The critical path is the longest path through the network that contains no float or slack. Any delays in the activities on the critical path will accordingly cause a delay in the project schedule.

3. Answer C. Time and cost estimates are interrelated; time estimates can impact cost and cost estimates can impact time too. All other statements are true.

4. Answer B. The project manager used analogous (or top-down) estimating. This is commonly used when a similar activity or project was completed in the past and when there is little information to start with.

5. Answer A. Rolling wave planning is a type of progressive elaboration in which you plan activities to the lowest level of detail needed to manage the work only when you start that particular phase. All the other options are invalid.

6. Answer B. This is an example of a mandatory dependency because software testing cannot commence without the setting up of the test environment.

7. Answer D. The Optimistic (30), Most Likely (35) and Pessimistic (45) estimates have been provided in the question. Using the 3-point estimate (P.E.R.T technique), the likely completion time can be computed as follows: (30+(4*35)+45)/6 = 35.83 Weeks.

8. Answer C. The team is 'breaking down work packages into smaller increments' – this phrase essentially defines the creation of activities. Milestones and deliverables occur at levels above the work package while a scope elaboration list is just a made-up term.

9. Answer B. Fast-tracking, by definition, allows some activities to be run in parallel at the cost of some added risk. All other options given are incorrect.

10. Answer C. Path Start-A-C-E-G-End (28 weeks) is the critical path, and therefore, has zero float. Refer the network diagram provided below to understand the various network paths.

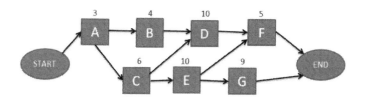

11. Answer A. There will be no change in the overall project schedule since Activity F is not on the critical path. A reduction in the duration of any activity (such as B or D) that is not in the critical path will have no impact on the overall project schedule too.

12. Answer B. The question asks what the change implies and not what should be done about it and therefore C and D are incorrect. There is no reason to assume that the project is no longer deliverable because compression techniques can be employed to adjust to the demand; therefore A is incorrect. The implication of the customer's demand is that the project now has a negative float of 2 weeks and therefore option B is the right choice.

13. Answer D. The change in activity B does not change the original critical path which is Start-A-C-E-F-End and therefore D is the correct answer choice. Refer original diagram below:

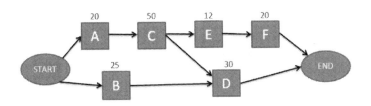

To avoid any confusion, always draw the network diagram to determine the critical path. You can see that 10 extra hours added to activity B (thereby making it 35 days from 25) will not impact the critical path.

14. Answer C. The schedule management plan is the most apt plan for this purpose as it contains details on how schedule changes will be managed. Other options are either invalid or not suited for the purpose.

15. Answer C. The Validate Scope process is carried out only at the time of monitoring and controlling and hence will not part of the current planning phase. Sequencing the activities has already been completed as it was mentioned that Dominic has prepared the network diagram. From the remaining two options, a schedule is an input to the risk management process and therefore has to be made before the risk management process. Hence, the next thing to do would be to create the preliminary schedule.

16. Answer C. Any activity on the critical path has zero float but this activity has a float of 9 (tested using LS – ES or LF – EF) and it is therefore not on the critical path. There is no information to judge whether the activity is having a lag or whether it is on schedule and hence, B and D are incorrect.

17. Answer C. It is already mentioned that there are no additional resources available and therefore crashing the project (option D) is not a viable option. Reducing the number of resources won't help complete the project earlier. Though removing an activity (option A) can be considered, since we know the activities are discretionary and risk is low, the best choice is to opt for fast tracking, or running activities in parallel, that is option C.

18. Answer C. Using a constant number of resources every month is an effect of resource levelling.

19. Answer D. Analogous estimates are top-down, high-level estimates, and they are therefore, less accurate than estimates obtained using bottom-up estimation techniques. Analogous estimating is not based on a detailed understanding of the work requirements and because of the limited information available it is unlikely to give clear indications to the project manager whether the project schedule is achievable. However, it does align the project team with the management's expectation on how long the project is supposed to take.

20. Answer C. Both these charts are used in planning. However, milestone charts are used in situations where fewer details are needed while bar charts are used when a greater amount of detail needs to be provided. This is why it is preferable to use bar charts for team members (who will appreciate the greater amount of detail) and milestone charts for management (as they would be more interested in the summary). Risk analysis could use both though it wouldn't be prudent to state one can substitute another for the purpose. Hence the best answer choice is C.

21. Answer C. While the existence of multiple critical paths MAY require more resources or COULD cost more, what we know for certain is that it increases project risk. The greater the number of critical paths, the greater the probability that if something goes wrong, project schedules will get impacted. Multiple critical paths also make project management more difficult.

22. Answer D. While taking the inputs of the client, the sponsor or Peter's manager may or may not be required, it is crucial to analyse risks associated with crashing each project activity.

23. Answer A. The beta standard deviation is calculated using the formula $(P-O)/6$ and therefore the standard deviation is $(20/14)/6 = 1$.

24. Answer A. The only output of the Control Schedule process from the answer choices is Change Requests. Updates to Organisational Process Assets (but NOT Enterprise Environment Factors) is an output of this process. Risk Register updates is not an output of the control schedule process and work performance information is an input to this process.

25. Answer D. A heuristic is a commonly accepted rule or practice, which is usually experience-based and not guaranteed to be optimal.

Knowledge Area 4 – Cost Management: Questions

1. A project manager is due to provide his project estimate within a day and he decides to use the Analogous Estimation technique for his project. What is a typical advantage associated with this technique?

    A.   It is a quick estimation technique.

    B.   It is very accurate.

    C.   It uses a detailed analysis of the project.

    D.   It gains an easy buy-in from project team members.

2. For any on-going project, what does a negative Cost Variance indicate?

    A.   The Earned Value currently exceeds the Planned Value.

    B.   The Planned Value currently exceeds the Earned Value.

C.   The Earned Value currently exceeds the Actual Cost.

D.   The Actual Cost currently exceeds the Earned Value.

3. A project manager has finished computing his project activities, work packages and project contingency reserve estimates. What would he have created as a result of having completed these three estimates?

A.   Definitive Estimate.

B.   Cost Baseline.

C.   Cost Budget.

D.   Bottom-up Estimate.

4. Following a Request for Proposal by an organisation, various vendors had submitted their proposals and the organisation's project manager chose the one who provided the cheapest solution. However, a year after the project was successfully closed and handed over to the maintenance team, it was evident that the operating cost of the solution was much higher than what the organisation had anticipated. What did the project manager probably miss that led to this situation?

A.   He didn't validate the vendor's credentials.

B.   He didn't conduct optimum quality testing.

C.   He didn't estimate life-cycle costing.

D.   He didn't do correct earned-value forecasting.

5. Which of the following statements best describes the Estimate at Completion (EAC)?

A.   It is the original amount of money budgeted for the project.

B. It is the original budget along with the contingency reserves.

C. It is the product of the Budget at Completion and the To-Complete Performance Index.

D. It is a budget forecast that takes the current project variances into account.

6. The project stakeholders of your new project have expressed concern over the size of the budget. You have coaxed them by telling that since a lot of the project is unknown, a progressive elaboration technique will be used and the current estimate covers a wide range of +/-45%. What type of estimate have you used?

A. Definitive Estimate.

B. Budget Estimate.

C. Rough Order Of Magnitude (ROM) Estimate.

D. Complex Estimate.

7. You are half-way through the implementation of a 1-year telecommunications project - the early launch of which will give your organisation a significant competitive advantage in the market. However, in the last stakeholder meeting, some stakeholders expressed concerns over the project going over budget and the possibility of a serious budget shortfall that could risk project completion. You are due for a project meeting later this week and you will need to brief stakeholders and address their concerns. Your project currently has an SPI of 1.2 and a CPI of 0.95 and your project is expected to progress at the current rate till completion. Which of the following responses would best address your stakeholders' concerns?

A. Inform the stakeholders the project team will take corrective action to bring the project budget back on track.

B. Inform the stakeholders the project, with its CPI of 0.95, is progressing well and is within the Definitive Budget range of +/-10%.

C. Inform the stakeholders the project team will consider scope reduction to cut costs without any delay.

D. Inform the stakeholders though there would be a minor cost increase by the time of completion, given the SPI of 1.2, the project will finish 8 weeks early, giving the company a much needed competitive advantage, which will ensure greater profitability in the long run.

8. There is a certain amount of money that is kept aside to cover known risks. Which of the following is the technique used to determine the amount of money that should be kept aside for covering these known risks?

A. Earned Value Management.

B. Reserve Analysis.

C. Estimate at Completion.

D. Variance Analysis.

9. A project manager needs to know the cost performance that must be achieved for the remaining work to complete the project within budget. Which of the following indexes will help him with this?

A. CPI.

B. EAC.

C.   TCPI.

D.   ETC.

10. Jacob is a project manager who is managing a 2-year, $4 Million project. At the end of the first year, he sees the project is 10% ahead of schedule, but is only yielding $0.9 for each dollar spent. He then gathers his project team to review the project and take suggestions on how to address the cost issue and bring it back on track. Which of the following would best address the cost issue he is facing?

   A.   As per one team member, Jacob should try fast-tracking to lower costs.

   B.   A business consultant suggested negotiating with the stakeholders to reduce the scope of delivery.

   C.   A senior technical resource suggested that since all complex technical work was complete, Jacob should swap some of the senior resources for less-experienced resources for the remaining duration.

   D.   A senior team member suggested dismissing all the contractors who were eating up one-fourth of the development budget to lower costs.

11. You have completed 6 months of a 1-year project you are managing. The project has a Budget-at-Completion (BAC) of $100,000 while Actual Cost (AC) is $60,000. If the Schedule Performance Index (SPI) of the project is 1.2, what is the Cost Performance Index (CPI)?

   A.   1.0

   B.   0.95

   C.   1.1

D. The CPI can't be determined from the given information.

12. A project manager is trying to identify ways of decreasing costs for his project. It would be best for him to look into which of these costs?

   A. Indirect and Direct Costs.

   B. Fixed Costs and Indirect Costs.

   C. Direct Costs and Variable Costs.

   D. Variable Costs and Fixed Costs.

13. Which of the following is the difference between the Cost Baseline and the Cost Budget?

   A. Management Reserves.

   B. Contingency Reserves.

   C. Cost account.

   D. Reserve Budget.

14. Which of the following is earned value measurement used for?

   A. Root cause analysis.

   B. Performance Reporting.

   C. Integration of project components.

   D. Project Plan creation.

15. While reviewing the earned value analysis of a project that was half-done, a stakeholder sees the CPI of the project was 0.75. Upon further investigation to understand why the CPI

was this low, he discovers that although the individual activity estimates add up correctly, something was amiss in the original project estimate. He later realises the discrepancy was because the project manager had used an analogous estimation technique. What could have probably averted the problem described?

A. SPI should have been used instead of CPI.

B. The history of previous projects should have been taken into account.

C. The CPI should have been measured using estimated costs.

D. A bottom-up estimation technique should have been used.

16. For a given project, the Budget at Completion is $9,500,000. Schedule Performance Index is 1.2, Actual Cost is $5,500,000 and Cost Variance is -$400,000 (negative). What is the Earned Value of the project?

A. $9,100,000.

B. $9,900,000.

C. $5,100,000.

D. $6,200,000.

17. During which of these processes is the Cost Baseline developed?

A. Estimate Costs.

B. Determine Budget.

C. Develop Schedule.

D. Plan Cost Management.

18. The following numbers for Earned Value, Planned Value and Actual Costs were captured every week, for 5 weeks in a row, for a given project.

Week	Earned Value	Planned Value	Actual Costs
1	$35000	$35,000	$36,000
2	$43,000	$45,000	$44,000
3	$55,000	$55,000	$57,000
4	$66,000	$65,000	$68,000
5	$72,000	$75,000	$79,000

What is the status of the project at the end of the fifth week?

A. It is ahead of schedule and over budget.

B. It is ahead of schedule and under budget.

C. It is behind schedule and over budget.

D. It is behind schedule and under budget.

19. A project has a budget of $1,200,000. Halfway through the project timeline, the earned value numbers were as follows: PV=$600,000, EV=$540,000 and AC = $660,000. If the project were to reach completion going at this same rate of progress, what is its Estimate at Completion (EAC)?

A. $1,080,000.

B. $1,466,666.

C. $1,200,000.

D. $1,320,000.

20. A post-mortem was done on a closed project. The SPI was 1.2 and the CPI was 0.85 at the time of closure. Which of the following statements is true?

    A.   The project was completed under budget and behind schedule.

    B.   The project was completed over budget and ahead of schedule.

    C.   The project was terminated early and at that time it was under budget and behind schedule.

    D.   The project was terminated early and at that time it was ahead of schedule but over budget.

21. A scope change for an existing project has been approved and this has increased the cost and the amount of work to be done. What impact will this have on the earned value data?

    A.   The scope change has made the earned value data analysis method redundant and it shouldn't be used anymore.

    B.   The project will become over budget because of the scope change as the earned value analysis is based on the original baseline.

    C.   The scope change will have no impact on earned value analysis.

    D.   The scope change will result in the cost baseline being adjusted and the new baseline will be used for calculating future earned value analysis.

22. Which of the following is the least likely to be captured in the Cost Management Plan at the time of its creation?

    A.   Methods for documenting cost.

B.   Level of accuracy needed for cost estimates.

C.   Rules for measuring cost performance.

D.   The budgets and their calculation.

23. For a new project, you have to setup new office space and buy some office furniture. What type of costs are these?

A.   Fixed Costs.

B.   Variable Costs.

C.   Overhead Costs.

D.   Opportunity Cost.

24. Which of the following cost estimating techniques is likely to be the most expensive?

A.   Analogous.

B.   Parametric.

C.   Bottom-up.

D.   Rough order of Magnitude.

25. What is the primary objective of using life cycle costing?

A.   To estimate any maintenance and operations costs.

B.   To estimate any installation and setup costs.

C.   To consider maintenance and operations costs in making project decisions.

D.   To estimate how long a product can be used before it can be discarded.

Knowledge Area 4 – Cost Management: Solutions

1. Answer A. Analogous (or top-down) Estimation is a quick estimation technique that draws on the previous experience of the project manager. However, it is a less accurate estimate and uses a less detailed analysis of the project unlike Bottom-up Estimation. It is less likely to gain an easy buy-in from project team members since they are typically not involved in the estimation process.

2. Answer D. The Cost Variance is calculated by the formula EV-AC and a negative CV means the Actual Cost incurred exceeds the Earned Value for that project and the project is over budget.

3. Answer B. The Cost Baseline is what is created taking into account the estimates for activities, work packages and the contingency reserve. A Cost Budget would need to take into account the management reserve on top of these too. While a Bottom-up Estimate focuses only on activities, a Definitive Estimate is an estimation range.

4. Answer C. In all likelihood, the project manager didn't estimate life-cycle costing which takes into account the total cost of the solution plus the maintenance and support cost for the entire lifetime of the solution.

5. Answer D. The Estimate at Completion is a formula used to calculate the total budget needed at project completion taking the current project variances into consideration. It can be computed by dividing the original BAC by the current CPI.

6. Answer C. The estimate range you have provided aligns best with the range of the ROM Estimate, which uses a range of +/- 50%. A Definitive Estimate has a variance of +/- 10% from the actual and a Budget Estimate has a range of -10% to +25% from the actual. There is no such thing as a Complex Estimate.

7. Answer D. Option A is a premature decision not needed at this point since the project is only marginally behind on costs and may self-correct. Option B, though technically correct, is a defensive answer that dismisses the stakeholder concerns. Scope reduction mentioned in Option 'C' is a last resort method for reducing costs and no evidence of other methods being discussed is provided; this isn't a wise response at this stage. Answer 'D' would be the most reassuring response because it shows the early finish time of 8 weeks will give a strong competitive advantage to the organisation, the benefits of which would boost profitability and would substantially offset the implications of a slightly over-budget project.

8. Answer B. Reserve Analysis is the technique that is specifically used to determine the risk contingency amount for a project.

9. Answer C. The To-Complete Performance Index is used to indicate the cost performance that needs to be achieved to meet the budget goal for any project.

10. Answer C. The best advice Jacob received is to swap the senior resources for more junior resources – while this will have a direct impact on the budget, it is unlikely to have any detrimental impact on the project because it was mentioned that complex technical work was complete. Fast-tracking is unlikely to reduce costs though it would compress the schedule. Reducing scope to meet costs is always a last option to adopt in case there is no other alternative. Also, dismissing all contractors blindly could have a severe impact on the project delivery.

11. Answer A. To determine the CPI in this question, the Earned Value (EV) needs to be determined first. Since we know SPI =1.2 and Planned Value (PV) = $ 50,000 (as 6 months have been completed), we can modify and use the formula SPI = EV/PV to determine the EV. Therefore, EV= SPI*PV = 1.2 * 50,000 = $60,000. The CPI can then be determined using the formula CPI = EV/AC = 60,000/60,000 = 1.

12. Answer C. It is unlikely that a project manager would have any control over Indirect Costs and Fixed Costs. Direct Costs on the other hand are costs that are directly connected to the project and Variable Costs are those costs that are based on the amount of activity accomplished on a project. These are the two costs he should therefore try to influence.

13. Answer A. The Cost Baseline comprises the Cost Account and the Contingency Reserves. The Cost Baseline along with the Management Reserves is called the Cost Budget. Reserve Budget is just a made up term.

14. Answer B. The primary objective of earned value measurement is to do forecasting and therefore, it is a great performance reporting tool that shows where a project currently stands in terms of budget and schedule.

15. Answer D. The problem here is that an analogous estimate was taken which only uses knowledge of previous projects and does not consider estimates of individual activities for the project that is being estimated for. While analogous estimates help in obtaining a quick estimate, it is the least accurate. In this case, the project turned out to be under-budgeted because of the analogous estimate; this in turn led to the CPI indicating the project as over-budget halfway through the project. If this project used a bottom-up estimation technique, a much more accurate budget could have been estimated and base-lined and subsequently this situation could've been avoided. None of the other options are correct – using SPI wouldn't have helped correct the cost estimate. Since the estimate was analogous, historic project information was already used and hasn't helped. The CPI is an index that by definition uses actual costs – not estimated costs and therefore this option too is incorrect.

16. Answer C. The Cost Variance = Earned Value – Actual Cost. Using this formula, we can find the Earned Value = Cost Variance + Actual Cost = (-400,000) + 5,500,000 = $5,100,000.

17. Answer B. The Cost Baseline is developed in the Determine Budget process.

18. Answer C. The SPI for Week 5 = 72000/75000 = 0.96 and CPI = 72000/79000 = 0.91; therefore the project is over budget and behind schedule.

19. Answer B. If the project were continue at the current rate till it completes, then the Estimate at Completion can be determined using the formula EAC= BAC/CPI or in other words EAC=BAC/(EV/AC) (Since CPI=EV/AC). Therefore, EAC = 1,200,000/ (540,000/660,000) = $146,666.

20. Answer D. The word 'post-mortem' indicates the project was terminated early and the CPI and SPI indexes clearly indicate the status at closure as being over budget and ahead of schedule.

21. Answer D. The approved scope change results in the adjustment of baselines (including cost baselines) and therefore the new earned value analysis will be calculated using the new cost baseline.

22. Answer D. The budgets are not calculated when preparing the Cost Management Plan; the budgets are only determined during the Determine Budget process which comes later.

23. Answer A. Office setup costs are always considered a type of Fixed Cost.

24. Answer C. A Bottom-up estimate requires complete project details and needs to be estimated starting from individual activities and upwards. This is therefore the most time-consuming and therefore, the most expensive.

25. Answer C. In order to make a sound decision on whether a project is feasible in the long run, it is prudent to estimate not just the project costs but also the subsequent maintenance and operations costs associated with the project.

Knowledge Area 5 – Quality Management: Questions

1. What does quality mean with respect to project management?

    A. Meeting management expectations.

    B. The degree of conformance to project requirements.

    C. Meeting or exceeding customer expectations.

    D. Staying within planned limits for the triple constraints.

2. The project management lifecycle comprises Initiating, Planning, Monitoring & Controlling and Closing. Which of the following is the cycle that is used as a basis for quality improvement?

    A. Preparation, Execution, Analysis & Action

    B. Initiation, Design, Observation and Verification

    C. Analysis, Review, Execution and Control

    D. Plan, Do, Check and Act.

3. A project manager has gathered all the issues on his project and ranked them by rate of occurrence and will use this information for his process improvement plan. What tool or technique has he used?

    A.   Pareto chart.

    B.   Statistical Sampling.

    C.   Ishikawa diagram.

    D.   Scatter diagram.

4. Your project sponsor wants to ensure that your project's end product will be of very high quality and is therefore willing to invest in quality improvements. However, he also places a caveat that the money invested in quality improvement should not result in the product becoming too expensive for the customer to buy. What do you call this process of comparing quality expense to the potential return-on-investment?

    A.   Marginal analysis.

    B.   Monte-Carlo analysis.

    C.   Process analysis.

    D.   Quality ROI.

5. You are facing an issue in a project you are managing. A product component routinely keeps breaking down even though the component was fixed each time it broke down earlier. A team member suggests that a root cause analysis needs to be done for the problem. Which of the following quality tools should you use in the given context?

    A.   Statistical sampling.

    B.   Ishikawa diagram.

C. Scatter diagram.

D. Pareto chart.

6. A control chart is one of the most useful tools used in Quality Management. Which of the following statements is incorrect with respect to control charts?

A. They can be used to measure whether a given process is stable.

B. They use control limits and specification limits.

C. The rule-of-seven is used to identify out of control processes plotted on control charts.

D. They can be used to measure process efficiency.

7. In order to prepare a quality management plan for your project, you request the PMO team to provide you with quality metrics you could use for documenting the plan. The PMO team then identifies past projects similar to your current project and informs you the quality metrics used in those projects would apply for your current project too. Which of the following techniques is being used here?

A. Statistical sampling.

B. Process analysis.

C. Benchmarking.

D. Process auditing.

8. In which of the following processes are quality policies and standards established?

A. Control Quality.

B. Plan Quality Management.

C. Perform Quality Assurance.

D. Develop Project Charter.

9. The quality testing team has identified and reported an out-of-control process in your project. Since the reported issue is a critical one, you have assembled your entire team in a meeting to get their inputs on how best to address this. In which of the following Project Management processes was this problem identified and what is it likely to result in?

A. Perform Quality Assurance process; Change Requests.

B. Control Quality process; Change Requests.

C. Perform Quality Assurance process; project management plan updates.

D. Control Quality process; quality management plan updates.

10. Of the various costs associated with Quality Management, cost of conformance is among the most important. Which of the following statements best describes cost of conformance?

A. It is the money spent to avoid failures.

B. It is the money spent because of internal failures.

C. It is the money spent for quality audits.

D. It is the money spent due to rework.

11. In a meeting with your project team, one of your software developers mentioned he is fine-tuning a deliverable and trying to analyse whether a sensitivity change will increase the accuracy of performance logging for that deliverable. Which of the following charts would best illustrate the cause and effect relationship mentioned in this case?

A. Ishikawa diagram.

B. Pareto chart.

C. Scatter diagram.

D. Control chart.

12. What is the purpose of control-limits in control charts?

A. To identify whether a process is in control or out of control.

B. To bring up process quality from 3 Sigma to 6 Sigma.

C. To show the range of acceptable results for a process.

D. To check whether the rule-of-seven pattern occurs in a control chart.

13. What is a Pareto chart supposed to highlight to an observer?

A. The standard deviation of variations in the observed process.

B. The minority processes that cause the majority of issues/problems.

C. The processes that repeatedly cause issues/problems.

D. The exceptions in process variations that need to be investigated further.

14. Which of the following techniques can be used by a project manager to perform quality assurance on his project?

A. Verification of Scope.

B. Code reviews.

C. Quality audits.

D. Manual inspection.

15. Which of the following statements is true regarding statistical sampling?

    A. It is commonly used in quality assurance to check whether samples conform to quality standards.

    B. It is used for verification of every item in a batch to determine whether the item can be accepted or rejected.

    C. It is used because examining all individual output items would consume too much time and cost too much.

    D. It is used for carrying out cause-effect analysis.

16. What are the various types of costs associated with Quality Management?

    A. Prevention costs, appraisal costs, and failure costs.

    B. Planning costs, doing cost, checking costs and acting costs.

    C. Planning costs, assurance costs, and control costs.

    D. Costs of good quality and costs of poor quality.

17. Which of the following is NOT a cost of non-conformance?

    A. Rework.

    B. Warranty cost.

    C. Quality training.

D. Defect replacement cost.

18. Which of the following is NOT a result of a quality audit?

A. New Process improvements.

B. Creation of quality metrics.

C. Confirmation of approved change request implementation.

D. Determination of whether project activities comply with organisational policies.

19. When analysing a control chart, a project manager notices 8 consecutive points above the mean. However, there is only one instance of such a pattern in that chart. What should the project manager do next?

A. Since there is only one instance, he can safely ignore the observation as a statistical anomaly.

B. He needs to find an assignable cause.

C. He needs to adjust the mean value slightly upward.

D. This is just a normal rule-of-seven observation and no action is needed.

20. A customer has expressed great satisfaction at the completion of a project. Three extra modules that weren't in the scope but were still delivered in the final product contributed to the customer's satisfaction. What does this mean in terms of project success?

A. The project was successful because the additional functionalities provided new knowledge areas for the team which would benefit in the long run.

B. The project was an unqualified success on account of customer satisfaction achieved.

C. The project was a failure because happy customers are a result of extra costs incurred.

D. The project was a failure because it was gold-plated.

21. A project manager, who is managing a new software project, is about to pro-actively work with the quality assurance department to ensure the project will meet the promised quality standards. Which of the following will they mandatorily need upfront before they start work on this process?

A. List of quality issues.

B. Quality control measurements.

C. Rework.

D. Quality improvement.

22. Which of the following statements correctly describes design-of-experiments (DOE)?

A. DOE determines what a quality outcome is.

B. DOE determines which variables will have the least impact on a quality outcome.

C. DOE determines which variables will have the most impact on a quality outcome.

D. DOE determines the R&D methodology that should be adopted.

23. Control charts used by many organisations often feature control limits that are +/- 3 sigmas from the mean. What

percentage of the population does this represent in a normal distribution bell curve?

A. 68.27%

B. 99.73%

C. 99.95%

D. 99.9999998%

24. It is often stated that quality has to be planned and not inspected in. Why is this so?

A. This improves quality and is less expensive than rework.

B. This reduces quality and is less expensive than rework.

C. This improves quality and is more expensive than rework.

D. This reduces productivity but is less expensive than rework.

25. Your organisation has invested a lot of time and money in adopting a lean production environment that uses the just-in-time principle. As a manager, this also means you will have to pay greater attention to supplies because the inventory maintained will now be reduced to:

A. Only about 5%.

B. Between 10-15%.

C. Between 15-20%.

D. 0%.

Knowledge Area 5 – Quality Management: Solutions

1. Answer B. Quality is the degree to which a project meets its requirements. It is not about meeting management or customer expectations or about staying within triple constraints.

2. Answer D. Plan, Do, Check and Act represent the correct cycle. The rest of the options are red herrings and incorrect answer choices.

3. Answer A. A Pareto chart is a common tool used to order issues by their rate of occurrence or frequency.

4. Answer A. Marginal analysis the process of examining the additional benefits of an activity compared to the additional costs incurred by that same activity. In this case, unless the cost incurred for quality improvement can be paid for by the customer, it may not be beneficial to make that improvement.

5. Answer B. The purpose of Ishikawa diagrams is to identify the causes leading to an effect (in this case, the component breakdown) and it is the right tool to use in the given context.

6. Answer D. Control charts cannot be used to measure the efficiency of a process. All other statements are true.

7. Answer C. Benchmarking is the technique in which key artefacts from previous projects are used for comparison and the given question describes an example of this technique.

8. Answer B. The quality policies and standards are established in the Plan Quality Management process.

9. Answer B. An out-of-control process will be identified in the Control Quality process and in order to rectify this problem, change requests are usually initiated.

10. Answer A. Cost of conformance is the money spent to avoid failures and includes the costs associated with various quality assurance activities.

11. Answer C. A scatter diagram that plots sensitivity on one axis and accuracy of performance logging on the other will best illustrate how a change in the former will impact the latter. Therefore, this is the best choice among the listed options.

12. Answer A. The purpose of control-limits is to identify whether a process is in control or out of control. It does not help bring up quality as suggested in Option B. Option C is incorrect because even though control-limits do show the range of acceptable results, their underlying 'purpose' is to use that range to determine whether process variations are within limit and therefore in control. Option D is incorrect because the rule-of-seven is just a way to identify a violation – the purpose of the chart isn't simply to identify this pattern.

13. Answer B. The Pareto principle specifies that 80% of problems are attributable to 20% of the causes or in other words imply the vast majority of problems are attributable to a minor number of causes –the Pareto chart accordingly highlights the minority causes that cause the majority of problems.

14. Answer C. As per PMBOK definition, a quality audit is a structured independent process to determine if project activities comply with organisational and project policies, processes and procedures. Accordingly, quality audits need to be carried out by the project manager to perform quality assurance on his projects.

15. Answer C. Statistical sampling involves examining limited samples of the output because examining all individual items would take too much time, cost too much or would be too destructive. It is done as part of the Control Quality process commonly (and is not associated with Quality assurance, as suggested in Option A). It is not used for carrying out cause-effect analysis (Option D) and isn't used for verifying every item in a batch (Option B).

16. Answer A. There are two major categories of quality costs – costs of conformance (they are further divided into prevention costs and appraisal costs) and costs of non-conformance (further divided into internal failure costs and external failure costs). Option A is the only option that captures these all these costs correctly.

17. Answer C. Quality training is a cost of conformance whereas all other three options provided are costs of non-conformance.

18. Answer B. Quality metrics are created in the Plan Quality Management process and act as an input to the Perform Quality Assurance process where quality audits are undertaken.

19. Answer B. The observation indicates that the rule-of-seven has been breached and the process is out of control (a single instance of the pattern is enough to indicate an out-of-control process). The project manager needs to find an assignable cause and then initiate corrective action.

20. Answer D. Delivery additional work/functionality outside the agreed scope is gold-plating, which costs both time and money and makes a project unsuccessful irrespective of customer satisfaction achieved.

21. Answer B. The process described in the question is Perform Quality Assurance and quality control measurements are an input to this process. While quality issues may lead to quality assurance efforts, the list of quality issues is not a mandatory input to the mentioned process. Quality improvement is an output of Perform Quality Assurance while rework is an output of the Control Quality process.

22. Answer C. DOE helps a project manager determine the variables that have the most impact on a quality outcome and therefore highlight the variables a project manager will need to focus his efforts on.

23. Answer B. The percentage represented by +/- 3 sigmas is 99.73. The percentage represented by +/- 1 sigma is 68.27 and that represented by +/- 6 sigmas is 99.999999.

24. Answer A. Adopting the pro-active approach of planning instead of inspecting helps define the appropriate level of quality required and that improves overall quality, productivity and is less expensive over the long when compared with the cost of non-conformance (such as rework).

25. Answer D. In a just-in-time environment, supplies are delivered only on a need-basis and therefore inventory maintained is 0%.

Knowledge Area 6 – Human Resources Management: Questions

1. Who came up with the motivational theory which states that people are most motivated by one of three primary needs - achievement, affiliation and power?

   A. Herzberg.

   B. Maslow.

   C. McClelland.

   D. McGregor.

2. A new project manager had his first team project meeting and during the meeting, his authority and his ability to effectively lead a team were questioned by some of the team members. Which of the following is the best type of project manager authority this project manager should possess to earn this team's respect and to get them on his side?

   A. Referent power.

   B. Legitimate power.

C. Penalty power.

D. Expert power.

3. Which of the following details is not captured in an issue log?

A. The issue owner.

B. The probability of occurrence.

C. The resolution.

D. The date on which added.

4. The Vice President of your department has just reviewed a project you had successfully closed as a project manager. He was particularly impressed by a team member who did some outstanding work as a developer. Therefore, the VP decides to promote him, on account of that work, to the position of a Testing Manager - a role that is currently vacant, and one which the VP believes can be suitably fulfilled by that team member. In management terms, this act is termed as:

A. The expectancy effect.

B. The Halo effect.

C. The promotion effect.

D. The transference effect.

5. In a project meeting with various stakeholders, the functional team leaders of the development and testing teams had a major disagreement on how to make up for lost time on the project. While one wanted the team to work an extra hour for the next five working days, the other wanted the team to come in an hour early for five days, to compensate for the lost time. When an hour had passed with neither party convincing the other, the VP finally interrupted and declared "Since you are not able to reach a consensus on this, I believe the best way

to sort this is to work this coming Saturday. You can inform your team members accordingly and proceed".

What was the type of conflict resolution approach adopted here?

    A.   Forcing.

    B.   Confronting.

    C.   Collaborating.

    D.   Compromising.

6. Tom is a program manager in your office who is a notorious workaholic. He is also sceptical about his subordinates all the while and believes he must constantly micro-manage the work of his subordinates to ensure their work is completed on time. What type of a project manager is Tom?

    A.   Theory X manager.

    B.   Theory Y manager.

    C.   Expectancy theory manager.

    D.   Achievement theory manager.

7. In a recent team project meeting, some of the stakeholders were clarifying doubts on the new product features that were being developed by the project team members. One of the stakeholders directed a question at a team member who seemed clueless on being asked the question and redirected it to the project manager. What did the PM most likely forget to prepare?

    A.   The staffing management plan.

    B.   The RACI matrix.

C. The resource breakdown structure.

D. The work breakdown structure.

8. Which of the following best describes what the responsibility assignment matrix depicts?

A. The reporting hierarchy of the team members.

B. The calendar availability of a resource for work.

C. The specific work and the due date of deliverables.

D. The ownership of project deliverables.

9. It has been two weeks since your project started and though many of your team members were frequently disagreeing and quarrelling to begin with, they have now started disagreeing much less and have started showing signs of gelling together as a team. While their performance hasn't peaked yet, you believe that in another week or two the team will perform much better and will hit maximum productivity. Which stage of the Tuckman ladder model is your team currently in?

A. Forming.

B. Storming.

C. Norming

D. Performing.

10. Which of the following is not a power derived from the project manager's position?

A. Expert power.

B. Formal power.

C. Reward power.

D. Penalty power.

11. A project manager, who is part of a matrix organisation, realises he needs additional human resources to carry out his project work. Who should he ideally request these resources from?

A. The PMO manager.

B. The functional manager.

C. The sponsor.

D. The project team.

12. Project priorities and schedules are two of the most common causes of conflicts on projects. Which of the below is the third most common cause?

A. Cost.

B. Management decisions.

C. Resources.

D. Differences in personality.

13. A fellow project manager has been frequently encountering conflicts on his team and he approaches you for advice. Which conflict management technique would you advise him to adopt for the most long-lasting solutions?

A. Compromising.

B. Withdrawing.

C. Smoothing.

D. Problem solving.

14. A project that is three quarters complete has an SPI of 1.02 and a CPI of 1.0. All deliverables made to the customer so far have been accepted without issues. The responsibility assignment matrix (RAM) hasn't changed since the project started and the project manager is expecting a smooth and successful closure of the project in due time. Both the sponsor and the customer are happy. However, despite the positives, there is a project team member who has been regularly complaining about the time consumed by the project. What would be the best thing the project manager could do in this situation?

A. Obtain a formal acceptance from the customer for deliverables.

B. Review the reward system in place for the project.

C. Improve the schedule performance of the project.

D. Explore options to extend the project schedule.

15. While managing a project team, both team performance assessments and project performance appraisals need to be carried out. The difference between the two is that, in team performance assessments, the primary focus is on:

A. Evaluating how well the project team as a whole is performing.

B. Evaluating how well individual team members in the project are performing.

C. Minimising the staff churn.

D. Team building efforts.

16. Which of the following options represent the various stages of team development, as per the Tuckman Ladder, in the right order?

A. Initialising, storming, collaborating, performing, and closing.

B. Forming, storming, norming, performing, and adjourning.

C. Directing, supporting, coaching, and delegating.

D. Forming, performing, storming, norming, and adjourning.

17. You have just been assigned as the project manager for a new project that will bring immense value to your organisation. However, you notice a high level of resistance to the project from many stakeholders right at the outset. What should you ideally do to address this problem?

A. Disengage from these stakeholders during key decision-making, and convey decisions to them after they have been made, thereby getting these stakeholders to support the project as they are left with no other alternative.

B. Create a responsibility assignment matrix (RAM) that will clearly outline the responsibilities of all stakeholders.

C. Organise a meeting with these stakeholders to present the project, establish ground rules and to understand the various organisational and personal issues and then get them involved in the project.

D. Create an organisational breakdown structure that will clearly outline the responsibilities of each department, including all the departments these stakeholders belong to.

18. Abigail is a new project manager who is planning human resource management for her project. She realises that a few of

the team members she will be working with aren't qualified enough for the tasks they will be performing despite being the only suitable candidates for those roles. What should be Abigail's course of action?

A. She should plan quality audits.

B. She should plan quality inspections.

C. She should develop a training plan.

D. She should look for other candidates.

19. The advantages of co-location for a project team are many. Which of the following is NOT an advantage of co-location?

A. Proximity to customer premises.

B. Reduction in travelling time and cost.

C. Improved communication between team members.

D. Same time zone and similar working hours for team members.

20. During the execution stage of his project, a project manager notices that a new team member has been isolated by the rest of the team. Nobody initiates a conversation with this new team member and the only person the team member speaks with during the entire course of the day is the project manager himself. Which of the following would be a wrong approach to address this situation?

A. Trying to obtain feedback from other team members individually to understand the situation.

B. Trying to obtain feedback from the isolated team member to understand the situation.

C. Not interfering since interpersonal relationships between team members are their private matter which they should sort on their own.

D. Incorporating team building measures to improve team cooperation and team effectiveness.

21. Gabriel is the project manager in a consulting firm who manages a team of highly skilled individuals. Since Gabriel's team members are well experienced, he seldom gets directly involved in their work but is available as and when any team member needs his input. Every week, the team members send across a progress update of the work they did and Gabriel reviews them to keep track of the work being completed. This kind of non-intrusive managerial style that Gabriel follows is termed:

A. Autocratic.

B. Coaching.

C. Directing.

D. Laissez-faire.

22. Rachel manages a project team of ten people and some of them occasionally have differences of opinion that can disrupt work. One Friday evening, she spots two of her team members having a spirited argument. Hamish, the tester, wanted to test a new software release on a computer with the Windows 8 platform, whereas Steve, the developer, wanted the same release to be tested on a computer with the Windows 10 platform. On further enquiry, Rachel got to know that Steve insisted on using Windows 10 to ensure compatibility as he carried out the development on the same platform. Hamish, on the other hand, insisted on using Windows 8 only because the computer he used for testing had the older Windows 8 platform and he didn't have access to another machine with Windows 10 installed on it. Rachel makes the necessary

arrangements for procuring a Windows 10 pre-installed computer for Hamish after which he agrees to carry out the testing on the Windows 10 platform. What kind of conflict management technique did Rachel employ in this situation?

A. Compromising.

B. Collaborating.

C. Smoothing.

D. Withdrawing.

23. Jacob manages a well acclaimed project team. All his team members are very committed and extremely productive because team members believe their commitment will be accounted for during the next performance appraisal and they will be given a fair bonus or a salary hike based on their effort, as it has happened always in the past. This belief among Jacob's team members is directly in-line with which motivation theory?

A. Maslow's Theory.

B. Expectancy theory.

C. Theory of X and Y.

D. Theory of Needs.

24. A project manager's on-going project hits a major roadblock when a key resource is pulled out from the project by his functional manager for another project which is of higher priority. Who among the following can best address the project manager's issue?

A. The project team.

B. The sponsor.

C. The management.

D. The customer.

25. Whose motivational theory talks about hygiene factors – the presence of which may not motivate an employee but the absence of which will demotivate an employee?

A. McClelland.

B. Maslow.

C. Herzberg.

D. McGregor.

Knowledge Area 6 – Human Resources Management: Solutions

1. Answer C. The theory of needs, as described in the question, was developed by David McClelland.

2. Answer D. Among all the five powers outlined in the PMBOK, expert and reward powers are considered the best. Expert power is considered a positive power that can influence team members and in this instance, if the project manager were to demonstrate expert power, he would be able to earn his team's respect.

3. Answer B. An issue is added to an issue log after it has already materialised (unlike a risk) and therefore, it doesn't make sense to capture the probability of its occurrence. All other options show fields that are usually part of an issue log.

4. Answer B. The tendency to expect a team member to do well in one sphere because he showed excellence in a different sphere is called the Halo Effect. All other options are made-up terms.

5. Answer A. The VP, in this case, resolved the conflict by forcing his decision on the team leaders.

6. Answer A. Tom is a classic example of a Theory X manager, in line with McGregor's Theory of X and Y. Such managers are more often than not doubtful of the commitment of subordinates and tend to micro-manage their work.

7. Answer B. The RACI matrix would have clearly stated who were responsible, accountable, consulted and informed for each of the product features that were developed. A missing RACI matrix would mean that other stakeholders wouldn't know who was responsible for a given component and therefore would be likely to direct questions on it to the wrong person.

8. Answer D. A responsibility assignment matrix (such as the RACI matrix) provides information on the project deliverables and their ownership. Option A refers to details in the resource breakdown structure, Option B refers to details in the resource calendar and Option C refers to details covered in the WBS dictionary.

9. Answer C. Your team has just completed the storming phase and is now in the norming phase where team members start building good working relationships.

10. Answer A. When somebody is legitimised as a project manager, he/she will acquire formal, reward and penalty powers. However, expert power (technical or non-technical) has to be earned.

11. Answer B. In matrix organisations, power is distributed between the project manager and the functional manager. Therefore, the project manager will need to negotiate with the functional manager if he needs additional resources.

12. Answer C. The top four reasons of conflicts are schedules, project priorities, resources and technical opinions. Cost, differences in personality and management decisions do not feature among the major reasons.

13. Answer D. Problem solving (or collaborating), is the longest lasting solution because it gets the buy-in from everybody involved and addresses the root cause of the conflict.

14. Answer B. The only real problem outlined in the question is that the project team member is complaining. The project is running on schedule as per the SPI and therefore there is no need to improve performance. Extending the schedule or obtaining a formal acceptance from customer will have no impact on the team member's dissatisfaction. Given the RAM hasn't changed since the commencement of the project, the team member's role and responsibilities would have remained the same throughout and therefore shouldn't be the cause of complaint as he would have agreed with these at the outset. The problem here could be a lack of motivation due to an ineffective reward system. Therefore, the best course of action, among the given options, would be to review the reward system for the project.

15. Answer A. In team performance assessments, the primary focus is on evaluating how well the project team, as a whole, is performing. On the other hand, in project performance appraisals, the primary focus is on evaluating the performance of individual team members.

16. Answer B. The various stages of team development, in right order, are: forming, storming, norming, performing, and adjourning.

17. Answer C. The issue here is the resistance from the stakeholders that could weaken their commitment to the project. This cannot be addressed by creating a RAM, or by creating an organisational breakdown structure, or by disengaging these stakeholders from decision-making. This issue can be addressed, however, by involving of all these stakeholders during project planning and decision making. Participation of team members and other stakeholders during planning adds their expertise to the process and also strengthens stakeholders' commitment to the project.

18. Answer C. If a project manager realises that the team members who are about to be assigned to a project do not have the required competencies needed for the project, a training plan can be developed as part of the project. This is the right course of action in the given context also, given that these are the only suitable candidates for the role.

19. Answer A. Co-location ensures project team members get to work together in one location but does not ensure proximity to customer premises or bring the customer any closer to the project team.

20. Answer C. Not interfering in the matter would be akin to withdrawing and would not address the issue in hand. Avoiding the problem could have long term repercussions on team productivity and this is therefore a wrong approach. All other options would either help the project manager understand the problem better (to address it subsequently) or help in improving team dynamics that could potentially sort the problem.

21. Answer D. A Laissez-faire manager is one who doesn't directly get involved in the work of the team but manages and consults only when necessary.

22. Answer B. The technique Rachel successfully used is collaborating (or problem solving). Rachel listened to both viewpoints, got to the root of the problem and subsequently addressed the underlying cause thereby leading to a win-win situation for both parties involved.

23. Answer B. The gist of the expectancy theory is that employees who believe their efforts will lead to effective performance, and who expect to be rewarded for their accomplishments, will remain productive as long as they are rewarded in line with their expectations.

24. Answer B. The sponsor is responsible for preventing undue changes to the project and determines priority between projects. Therefore, the project manager should approach the sponsor for this concern.

25. Answer C. Herzberg's theory deals with hygiene factors and motivating agents.

Knowledge Area 7 – Communications Management: Questions

1. You have just made a presentation of your project's status to the senior management team. What kind of communication is this?

    A.   Formal verbal.

    B.   Informal verbal.

    C.   Formal written.

    D.   Informal written.

2. You called a team-member to ask whether the user interface testing had commenced. He replies "the user interface testing? Yes, it had started yesterday." What kind of communication was used in this situation?

    A.   Paralingual.

    B.   Non-verbal.

    C.   Feedback.

D. Passive listening.

3. Two new team members have been added to a project team which earlier had 8 members, including the project manager. How many extra lines of communication have been added?

    A. 28

    B. 45

    C. 73

    D. 17

4. Which of the following is variance analysis used for?

    A. Statistical modelling.

    B. Comparing actuals with baseline figures.

    C. Budget forecasting.

    D. Status reporting.

5. You have noticed that a key member of your project team, a senior developer who is usually very diligent at work and who commands immense respect from the rest of the team, has not been himself of late. He has been reclusive most of the time, has been appearing late for work and has also been slipping on various work packages he was assigned to work on. You believe he might be facing personal or health issues that are having an adverse impact on his work performance and you would like to get to the bottom of the problem. What should be the ideal method of communication you should be using initially to address this issue?

    A. Formal written.

    B. Informal written.

C.   Formal verbal.

D.   Informal verbal.

6. Which of the following is not an output of the Control Communications process?

A.   Work performance information.

B.   Work performance data.

C.   Project management plan updates.

D.   Change requests.

7. You need to conduct training for some of your team members. Since your team members are spread across the globe and in different time zones, you decide the best way to conduct this would be by using an e-learning system the team members can access and use for learning as per their convenience. What kind of communication method is this?

A.   Push method.

B.   Pull method.

C.   Interactive method.

D.   Collaborative method.

8. Which of the following details are not captured in the communication management plan?

A.   Stakeholder communication requirements.

B.   Person responsible for communicating the information.

C.   Person or group who will receive the information.

D.   Responsibility assignments.

9. Which of the following is not generally considered a part of active listening?

   A.   Interrupting as and when required.

   B.   Maintaining eye contact.

   C.   Paraphrasing.

   D.   Interpreting the information.

10. Which of the following statements accurately describes the main purpose of the communications management plan?

   A.   It is mainly focussed on the various communication technologies to be used by the project management team.

   B.   It is not a constituent of the project management plan.

   C.   It describes the various information delivery needs, the required format, and the necessary level of detail.

   D.   It describes the rules to be followed while communicating in cross-cultural teams.

11. Ravi's project team has undergone some recent changes after his project's priority was changed. Two of the senior testers were replaced by three junior testers. Ravi's team now has eight team members in total (including him) after this change. What is the change in the number of communication lines?

   A.   It has increased by 7.

   B.   It has decreased by 7.

   C.   It has increased by 21.

D.   It has decreased by 21.

12. Which of the following qualities of team leadership is the most important for a project manager?

   A.   Team building expertise.

   B.   Technical expertise.

   C.   Communication skills.

   D.   Time management skills.

13. John, the project manager of a multi-national IT corporation, was due to send a status report on the 15th of the month. As a part of the report, he was to include some performance statistics which were to be collected and provided by a team member, Oliver, who was working at the overseas client location. Unfortunately, Oliver emails the details exactly a day late resulting in John's report being sent late too. John later calls up Oliver and enquires about the reason for the delay. A surprised Oliver replies, "But when you called, you told me you needed the data by 10 am on the 16th and I had sent it across just before 10 am on the 16th". John retorts; "But I'm certain I said the 15th and not the 16th because the 16th is a Saturday". Oliver thinks for a moment and then replies, "Oh, I'm sorry John but I must have heard it wrong then. I really thought you said the 16th; the line wasn't that clear and I was straining to hear what you said".

What could have been done to avoid this problem?

   A.   Feedback should have been used during the conversation.

   B.   The details should have been captured in an issue log after the call.

   C.   Oliver should have paid better attention to the call.

D. Paralingual communication should have been used.

14. The presence of communication blockers is mostly likely to cause which of the following:

A. Management displeasure.

B. Conflicts.

C. Better team dynamics.

D. Project delays.

15. Jamie is a project manager who is due to send a project report to his management team on Friday. However, on Friday afternoon, the office that Jamie works in faces a temporary network issue and he therefore sends the report via FAX instead of email. What kind of communication did Jamie use in this instance?

A. Interactive.

B. Push.

C. Pull.

D. Written.

16. During a formal project review meeting held at the client premises on a Monday morning, one of your team members enters the meeting wearing a T-shirt and jeans, whereas everybody else had turned up dressed in formals. On seeing this team member in casual attire, other team members raised their arms and eyebrows in a questioning way. What kind of communication was used here?

A. Paralingual.

B. Feedback.

C.   Active listening.

D.   Non-verbal.

17. A communication management plan helps a project manager define the approach to communicate both efficiently and effectively. What is meant by efficient communication?

    A.   Providing only the information that is needed.

    B.   Providing information in the right format, at the right time, and with the right impact.

    C.   Providing information very quickly.

    D.   Providing information only to the important stakeholders.

18. While pull communication is effective in many situations, it has its own disadvantages too. Which of the following is a major disadvantage of pull communication?

    A.   The quantity of information provided through pull communication is too much.

    B.   The information provided through pull communication is customised as per every user's needs.

    C.   Pull communication is ineffective if stakeholders don't participate in the system.

    D.   Pull communication is not useful for the management.

19. Noise is a part of the communication model. Identify an example of noise from the below.

    A.   Lack of attention by a stakeholder during a status meeting.

B. Smudges and marks on printed reports that make the reports hard to read.

C. A manager who overlooks an important clause in a contract.

D. A message sent to the wrong recipient.

20. John is managing a development project and his customer has asked for some scope change in the proposed architecture. What's the most apt form of communication for John to use in this situation?

A. Informal written.

B. Formal written.

C. Informal verbal.

D. Formal verbal.

21. Jacob's project will result in a billing product that will be used in his customer's regional offices in China, Japan, and Saudi-Arabia. Jacob therefore gets the product manual translated into Mandarin, Japanese and Arabic so that the users working in these offices can understand the manual. What is Jacob doing when he gets this communication translated?

A. Decoding.

B. Encoding.

C. Active listening.

D. Effective listening.

22. You meet a project stakeholder in the corridor and ask her how the project is progressing. She replies rhetorically in a sarcastic high-pitched voice "the project is progressing so well.

Isn't it?" Which of the following best describes the communication that the stakeholder used?

    A. Paralingual.

    B. Non-verbal.

    C. Active listening.

    D. Feedback.

23. Which of the following is NOT an example of active listening?

    A. A listener repeating what he heard to make sure he understood it right.

    B. A listener asking for questions when he didn't understand what was said.

    C. A listener checking project emails while attending a presentation.

    D. A listener nodding in agreement in response to the speaker.

24. Which of the following is NOT an input to the Manage Communications process?

    A. Communications management plan.

    B. Work performance reports.

    C. Enterprise environmental factors.

    D. Project communications.

25. Which of the following information is LEAST likely to be captured in a communications management plan?

A. Stakeholder communication requirements.

B. Methods and technologies to be used for communicating information.

C. Any risks associated with communication.

D. Communication constraints.

Knowledge Area 7 – Communications Management: Solutions

1. Answer A. Presentations made as part of the project are considered formal verbal communication.

2. Answer C. The team member repeated the question and then responded. This is a very good example of feedback.

3. Answer D. Do note that the question does not ask for the total number of communication lines but only the increase in the number of communication lines. The current number of members in the project team is 10 and the previous number was 8. If 'n' represents the number of team members, the number of communication lines can be computed using the formula $[n*(n-1)]/2$. Therefore, the number of extra lines of communication can be computed using the formula $(10*9)/2 - (8*7)/2 = 17$.

4. Answer B. Variance analysis, by definition, is used for comparing actuals with baselines.

5. Answer D. In the given context, the first step is to have an informal off-line chat with the team member to assess the situation – in other words, you need to use informal verbal communication. Formal communication would be premature at this point and using informal written communication would eliminate non-verbal cues making the communication less effective.

6. Answer B. Work performance data is an output of the executing process group and is an input to the Control Communications process.

7. Answer B. All E-learning systems fall under the pull method category because the user needs to 'pull' information from the system as and when required.

8. Answer D. Responsibility assignments are part of the responsibility assignment matrix and are not captured in the communication management plan.

9 Answer A. Interrupting when the message is being conveyed is not considered a part of active listening.

10. Answer C. The communications management plan is primarily used to capture the various information delivery needs, the required format and the necessary level of detail required with respect to communication for the project.

11. Answer A. The total number of team members in the team is currently 8 and had previously been 7. Therefore, the net change in number of team members is 1. Accordingly, the previous number of communication channels were $[7*(7-1)]/2$ = 21 and the current number of communication channels is $[8*(8-1)]/2$ = 28. Therefore, the number of communication channels has increased by 28-21 = 7.

12. Answer C. While all the skills and expertise mentioned in the answer choices are valuable, the most valuable team leadership quality among the lot is the ability to communicate well. A project manager spends 90% of his time communicating; therefore, he has to be an excellent communicator first and foremost.

13. Answer A. Since the line itself wasn't clear, Oliver could have mentioned about the lack of line clarity during the call and then repeated the requirement back to John to cross-check what he heard. This could've avoided the problem. There was no issue to be captured in the log, and paralingual communication wouldn't have made much of a difference since the problem was with the medium. Likewise, Oliver had mentioned he was straining to listen so there is no reason to believe Oliver paying better attention would have helped the cause either.

14. Answer B. Communication blockers (or miscommunications) are most likely to result in conflicts between the various stakeholders involved.

15. Answer B. Both email and FAX are examples of push communication.

16. Answer D. Communication using facial expressions and gestures is a part of non-verbal communication.

17. Answer A. As per the PMBOK, efficient communication means providing only the information that is needed while effective communication means providing information in the right format, at the right time, and with the right impact.

18. Answer C. Pull communication requires a user to access a particular system or resource (example website/repository) to obtain information and therefore, if a stakeholder doesn't participate in this process, he/she will not receive the necessary information.

19. Answer B. Noise is something that interferes with communication and therefore, smudges and markings that make printed reports difficult to read are examples of noise. None of the other options are examples of noise.

20. Answer B. The most apt form of communication to use for formal scope changes is formal written communication.

21. Answer B. Modifying the message for the recipient to understand is referred to as encoding.

22. Answer A. In paralingual communication, the tone and pitch of the voice are used to convey information in addition to the words spoken.

23. Answer C. The listener is multi-tasking and is not engaged in active listening. All other options describe features of active listening.

24. Answer D. Project communications is an output of the Manage Communications process and is not an input to this process.

25. Answer C. The communications management plan is least likely to capture any associated risks as these would be captured in a risk register. All other options capture information that is part of the communications management plan.

Knowledge Area 8 – Risk Management: Questions

1. You are a project manager who needs to identify various risks associated with your new project. Therefore, you call a meeting of all your team members and ask them to share their ideas regarding potential project risks. A facilitator you have appointed collates all the ideas that emanate in the meeting and later provides these to you to add to your risk register. What information gathering technique did you use here?

    A.   The Delphi technique.

    B.   Brainstorming.

    C.   Interviews.

    D.   Assumptions analysis.

2. During the Identify Risks process, you and your team have identified over 250 project risks. However, performing quantitative risk analysis on all these risks will consume a massive amount of time and given that not all these risks are relevant, you would be unable to justify the time and resources

spent on such an activity. What should be your next course of action in this situation?

A. Use qualitative risk analysis as a way of prioritising risks for further action such as quantitative risk analysis.

B. Determine the probability of all these risks and then conduct quantitative analysis on those with high probability.

C. Determine the impact of all these risks and then conduct quantitative analysis on those with high impact.

D. Determine the risk triggers of all these risks and then conduct quantitative analysis on those for which triggers could not be identified.

3. There are various techniques used for identifying risks in the Identify Risks process. Which of the following is an output of the Identify Risks process?

A. Risk management plan.

B. Risk register.

C. Project management plan update.

D. OPA updates.

4. Ralph is a project manager working on a construction project who believes his client is very likely to propose some additional scope halfway through the project. If that were to happen and if the scope were to receive approval, Ralph would not be able to acquire enough resources to take up the additional scope in the required timeframe. Therefore, Ralph goes ahead and recruits 5 more people into his team as a pre-emptive measure. This action of his creates a new risk – if the

anticipated new scope doesn't materialise, the new team members will need to be paid from the existing project budget and that would affect the project's profitability. What kind of risk is this?

A. Residual risk.

B. Secondary risk.

C. Shared risk.

D. Enhanced risk.

5. Which of the following is not a tool/technique for performing quantitative risk analysis?

A. Reserve analysis.

B. Sensitivity analysis.

C. Expected monetary value.

D. Monte Carlo analysis.

6. Rose is a project manager who needs to carry out risk management. She is searching for a tool or technique to help her list out the various categories and subcategories of risks. Which of the following is the tool/technique that will suit her need?

A. Probability and impact matrix.

B. Risk breakdown structure.

C. Stakeholder matrix.

D. Quantitative risk analysis matrix.

7. What action should be taken on risks that are added to the watchlist?

A. They should be provided to the customer.

B. They should be kept aside as they are already accounted for in the contingency budget.

C. They should be revisited during the Monitoring and Controlling phase.

D. They should be added to the OPA as historical references for future projects.

8. A given project has a 70% potential of making a $50,000 profit and a 30% chance of making a $50,000 loss. What is this project's EMV?

A. +$20,000

B. -$20,000

C. +$50,000

D. -$35,000

9. What is the purpose of carrying out an assumptions analysis?

A. To identify root causes of risks.

B. To measure the effectiveness of planned risk responses.

C. To measure the validity of risk assumptions.

D. To identify historical information of risks.

10. Rebecca is managing a critical project which has several senior stakeholders from her organisation. Most of her project team members are experienced senior consultants who have carved a niche for themselves and were chosen carefully because of their high levels of technical expertise in their roles.

Recently, Rebecca had organised a team meeting after her sponsor decided to narrow the project scope due to budget constraints. The objective of the meeting was to get the team members' opinions on which of the originally planned deliverables could be excluded following the narrowing of the scope. But the meeting didn't go according to expectations because the team members vehemently disagreed with each other. The meeting was eventually dismissed after an hour as it had become a mere shouting contest and wasn't making any progress. What risk tool could have been used by Rebecca to avoid this situation?

    A.   SWOT analysis.

    B.   Delphi technique.

    C.   Brainstorming.

    D.   Nominal group technique.

11. A risk has just been triggered on your project. What is the usual (or most common) risk response to a triggered risk?

    A.   Workaround response.

    B.   Contingency response.

    C.   Mitigation response.

    D.   Avoidance response.

12. What is the purpose of using Monte-Carlo analysis? Choose the best answer:

    A.   To estimate the duration of an activity.

    B.   To estimate quality issues for a project.

    C.   To estimate the resource requirement.

D. To gain a better understanding of overall risks involved in a project.

13. Which of the following is NOT a key component in the risk register?

A. Date of identification.

B. Risk owner.

C. Risk priority.

D. Name of the person who identified the risk.

14. Your project is ready to move into the maintenance and support phase. However, you know the penalties associated with a service level agreement (SLA) breach is quite steep and your organisation's inexperienced maintenance team is likely to breach SLAs from time to time till they gain more experience. Therefore, you convince your management to source the maintenance activity to a more experienced third-party organisation and then proceed to sign an agreement with the third-party vendor to maintain the same SLAs you have in place with your customer. The agreement with the third-party organisation also includes the same penalty clauses you have with your customer. What kind of risk response strategy have you employed here?

A. Mitigation.

B. Transfer.

C. Share.

D. Accept.

15. During the course of a project, a risk materialises that was neither anticipated nor captured in the comprehensive risk register the project manager had earlier prepared after discussing with this team members. In order to handle the

emergency, a temporary fix was implemented till the time the problem could be studied in depth and a permanent resolution could be put into place. This response can be best called:

A. A workaround risk response.

B. A contingency risk response.

C. A secondary risk response.

D. A residual risk response.

16. During the course of your project, a risk materialises and your team implements the appropriate risk response strategy successfully. What should be the next thing you should do as a project manager?

A. Perform a risk reserve analysis to determine the remaining reserves.

B. Update the risk register.

C. Update the stakeholder management plan.

D. Inform the management team.

17. Which of the below is NOT a reason to perform risk management on a project?

A. To keep a track of opportunities.

B. To reduce the impact of threats.

C. To plan responses for known or unknown events.

D. To eliminate issues.

18. Which risk management process has watchlist as an output?

A. Plan Risk Management.

B. Perform Qualitative Risk Analysis.

C. Perform Quantitative Risk Analysis.

D. Plan Risk Responses.

19. Halfway through a project, a project manager discovers a new risk which could probably delay the completion of the project. What should be his next course of action?

A. He should qualify the risk.

B. He should inform the sponsor of the risk.

C. He should accept the risk.

D. He should develop a workaround.

20. In which project management process is a workaround determined?

A. Identify Risks.

B. Perform Quantitative Risk Analysis.

C. Plan Risk Responses.

D. Control Risks.

21. A contingency reserve was assigned to a risk that was identified on a project. Which type of risk response strategy is used when a contingency reserve is assigned to a risk?

A. Active risk acceptance.

B. Active risk mitigation.

C. Passive risk acceptance.

D.   Passive risk mitigation.

22. A project manager, assigned to a high-value software project in a rapidly evolving domain, used his own experience to chart out a risk management plan and identified risks which he documented in a risk register. He then analysed the risks and planned responses for these risks, which he then updated in the register accordingly. Nevertheless, during the course of the project, whenever risk control meetings were conducted, it became evident that these documents weren't very helpful. What had the project manager done wrong?

A.   He did the planning processes alone.

B.   He did not identify the risk triggers.

C.   He did not use a risk breakdown structure.

D.   The EMV calculations he made were incorrect.

23. What is a tornado diagram used for?

A.   To compare the relative importance of variables those have a high degree of uncertainty with those with less uncertainty.

B.   To compare the extent to which project deliverables meet stakeholder requirements.

C.   To compare team members on basis of their productivity.

D.   To rank and compare the various project risks after estimating their probability and impact.

24. In which situation is passive risk acceptance acceptable as a risk response strategy?

A.   When it is not possible to analyse the risk.

B. When the probability of occurrence of the risk is very low.

C. When the risk trigger cannot be identified.

D. When it is best to deal with that risk as it occurs.

25. What is the difference between management reserves and contingency reserves?

A. Management reserves are used to manage unknown events while contingency reserves are used to manage known risks.

B. Management reserves are used to manage known events while contingency reserves are used to manage unknown risks.

C. Management reserves are used to manage high priority risks while contingency reserves are used to manage low priority risks.

D. Management reserves are used to manage low priority risks while contingency reserves are used to manage high priority risks.

26. There are various risk response strategies for both opportunities and threats. Which of the following is a risk response strategy that is common to both these types of risks?

A. Exploit.

B. Transfer.

C. Share.

D. Accept.

27. At every project milestone, a project manager re-examines the risk register to identify any new risks, to ensure the risks in

his register are still relevant, and to close any risks that are no longer relevant. What is this technique used by the project manager called?

A. Risk audit.

B. Reserve analysis.

C. Risk reassessment.

D. Trend analysis.

28. The new office premises did not have sufficient parking space and the project manager found that he could rent a nearby vacant plot in order to procure the necessary parking space for his team members. However, this vacant lot was much larger than required and renting only a part of the property was not an option given by its owner. The project manager then heard that another office in the vicinity was short of office space too. He got in touch with a representative from that office and struck a deal to jointly rent the parking space. This resulted in cost savings for both his organisation and the other organisation. What type of risk did the manager face and what was his response strategy?

A. The manager faced a threat which he successfully mitigated.

B. The manager faced an opportunity, which he shared.

C. The manager faced an opportunity, which he accepted.

D. The manager faced a threat, which he successfully exploited.

29. What is the purpose of determining risk tolerances?

A. To help the team schedule project activities.

B. To help the team rank the project risks.

C. To measure the impact of various risks.

D. To help the project manager estimate project activities.

30. A project manager is sitting with his team and creating a risk response plan for identified risks. However, he realises that each time a risk response is planned for a risk, a secondary risk is also identified. What should the project manager do? Choose the best option.

A. Discard all the identified risks and start identifying risks from the beginning as this was not done properly the first time.

B. Document the secondary risks, continue with the risk response planning and later plan the responses to the secondary risks also.

C. Bring more people for the risk response planning process.

D. Spend more time and provide a more elaborate risk response for each risk.

Knowledge Area 8 – Risk Management: Solutions

1. Answer B. The technique described wherein various team members get together and bring forth all their ideas, which are then collated by a facilitator is called brainstorming.

2. Answer A. Your next course of action should be to perform qualitative risk analysis by accessing and combining their probability of occurrence and impact, in order to prioritise risks for further action. Using either probability or impact as a solo criterion for further action is incorrect because there could be high probability issues of low impact and vice versa. Selecting only such risks that lack risk triggers to perform quantitative analysis is also incorrect because that criterion alone gives no indication of priority, probability or impact of these individual risks.

3. Answer B. The risk register is the only output of the Identify Risks process. The risk management plan (which is a constituent of the project management plan also) is an output of the Plan Risk Management process whereas OPA updates is an output of the Control Risks process.

4. Answer B. Secondary risks are those risks that arise from a response to another risk. In this case, the new risk came up because Ralph dealt with the risk of not having resources on time in the event of new project scope being added.

5. Answer A. Reserve analysis is not a tool for performing quantitative risk analysis. It is a technique used as part of the Control Risks process to keep a tab on the contingency reserve and to determine whether the existing reserve is adequate for the amount of risk remaining.

6. Answer B. The risk breakdown structure (RBS) is a tool used for listing out the various categories and subcategories of risks in a given project.

7. Answer C. The documented items in the watchlist need be revisited from time to time to ensure noncritical items on the list have not become critical.

8. Answer A. The EMV of the project is calculated by the formula probability x impact. A profit will be considered as positive and loss as negative. Therefore the overall EMV in this case is 0.7* $50,000 – 0.3*50000 = +$20,000.

9. Answer C. Assumptions analysis is used to measure the validity of risk assumptions for the various risks identified for a project.

10. Answer B. Rebecca had used a brainstorming session which was shown to be failure. She could have used the Delphi technique in which opinion could've been sought from each of these experts anonymously - this would have removed the emotional components of the issue faced (prevalent in a live meeting) and these experts could've provided their opinion focussing only the facts and objectives.

11. Answer B. The most common response to a triggered risk is the execution of the contingency response which had been planned for.

12. Answer D. Monte-Carlo analysis uses a mathematical simulation model that runs numerous simulations to identify the range of possible outcomes for given scenario (risks) and can provide a better overview of overall project risk. It is not directly involved in estimation of activity duration, quality issues or resource requirements.

13. Answer D. Who identified the risk is not a key component in the risk register. The date of identification, risk owner and priority are all key components in the risk register.

14. Answer B. By signing up with a third-party vendor to do the maintenance activity using a similar agreement you have with your customer, you have effectively transferred the risk to the third-party vendor.

15. Answer A. The response to an unexpected negative risk that wasn't captured during risk planning is called a workaround response; it is usually a temporary solution put into place till a more permanent fix can be planned and implemented.

16. Answer B. The next thing to do after implementing the risk response strategy should be to update the risk register and keep it up-to-date. The risk reserve analysis will need to be done following this. Updating the stakeholder management plan or informing management may or may not be required.

17. Answer D. Issues are not risks but are situations that have already materialised and therefore their elimination is not covered under risk management. Opportunities are positive risks that need to be tracked, and reducing the impact of threats and planning risk response are objectives of risk management.

18. Answer B. The watchlist comprises low priority risks that were determined to be of too low impact and too low probability in the Perform Qualitative Risk Analysis process.

19. Answer A. The first action a project manager needs to carry out after identifying a new risk is to qualify/analyse it – doing so will help a project manager determine how to take it forward. The risk should be discussed with the sponsor only after analysing it. Developing a workaround does not apply here since workarounds apply to risks which were already triggered. A risk response strategy, such as accepting the risk, cannot be determined till the risk is qualified and hence is not a correct answer choice either.

20. Answer D. Workarounds are responses to risks that were not planned for or captured in the risk register. Therefore, if such a risk has materialised, then the project must be in the Control Risks process.

21. Answer A. Establishing a contingency reserve, including time, money or resources to handle the risk is a common active acceptance strategy. Acceptance strategies are used when it isn't cost effective to address a specific risk in any other way.

22. Answer A. The risk management documents weren't helpful because the project manager created the planning documents on his own and may have missed risks which were not evident to him. Expert judgement of other stakeholders such as senior management, the project team members, or SMEs, would have helped make the documents more comprehensive, and thereby, more useful.

23. Answer A. Tornado diagrams are used for carrying out sensitivity analysis and to understand how variations in project's objectives correlate with variations in different uncertainties.

24. Answer D. Passive risk acceptance is an accepted risk strategy in situations wherein it is not cost-effective or possible to address a risk in any other way and it would be best to deal with that risk as it occurs.

25. Answer A. Contingency reserves, which are estimated during the Perform Quantitative Risk Analysis process, are meant for addressing the identified risks. Management reserves, which are estimated when performing cost management, are meant to be used if any previously unforeseen event takes place.

26. Answer D. 'Accept' is a risk response strategy that can be adopted for both negative risks (threats) and positive risks (opportunities).

27. Answer C. The technique described in the question is risk reassessment and it is part of the Control Risks process.

28. Answer B. The project manager was faced with a positive risk (opportunity) and he chose to share this risk as a response strategy.

29. Answer B. Risk tolerances reflect the degree of risk the organisation will withstand and it is useful in ranking or prioritising the various project risks.

30. Answer B. Identifying secondary risks are also a part of the Plan Risk Responses process. The right approach in this situation is to document the secondary risks, continue with the risk response planning and to plan the responses to the secondary risks too.

Knowledge Area 9 – Procurement Management: Questions

1. In which of the following contract types does the buyer have least cost risk?

A. Firm Fixed Price.

B. Time and Materials.

C. Cost Plus Fixed Fee.

D. Cost Plus Award Fee.

2. In which process does a contract negotiation take place?

A. Plan Procurement.

B. Conduct Procurement.

C. Control Procurement.

D. Closure Procurement.

3. Jamie is the managing director of a startup that provides innovative software solutions for MNCs. Jamie's sales team had recently conducted a demonstration of their company's flagship product for a potential buyer. This potential buyer was extremely impressed by the product and following further discussions, issued a letter of intent (LOI) to purchase this product within two months. However, when Jamie tried to present this LOI to a banking firm to obtain some short-term loans for his organisation, the banking firm declined him outright without even going through the details of the LOI. The finances of the buyer organisation were sound, and Jamie's organisation had no history of bad debt. What could have been the MOST probable reason why the firm declined Jamie's request?

    A.   The potential revenue indicated by the LOI wasn't sufficient to cover the loan.

    B.   The LOI isn't legally binding.

    C.   The banking firm didn't approve of the buyer.

    D.   The banking firm didn't approve of the company's product.

4. What is an RFP?

    A.   An output of the Control Procurement process.

    B.   An output of the Plan Procurement process.

    C.   A tool/technique used in the Conduct Procurement process.

    D.   An output of the Close Procurement process.

5. Which of the following is LEAST likely to be true with respect to single source suppliers?

    A.   The buyer gets exactly what he needs.

B. The procurement process is simplified.

C. The buyer and seller have a well-established relationship.

D. The buyer gets the best possible price.

6. Which of the following is not a tool/technique of the Control Procurements process?

A. Procurement performance review.

B. Record management system.

C. Negotiations.

D. Claims settlement.

7. Your company is in discussions to purchase an innovative and unique software product from a small but reputed organisation. The product implementation may take about 6 months but this product will give your organisation a strong competitive edge over its competitors. However, there have been talks of the supplier organisation facing financial turmoil and rumours have it that it may go out of business very soon. You are worried that your company might lose its investment if the supplier goes out of business after project commencement. In order to protect its investment, your company had even proposed to buy the source code of the supplier company's product – which the supplier company declined. If the supplier company's survival is not guaranteed, what the best thing your company could do to protect its interests?

A. Set up a code escrow agreement with the supplier.

B. Abandon the discussions and look for another supplier.

C. Try to buy the supplier company itself.

D.   Force the company to sell the source code.

8. Which form of contract would be the best choice for a buyer organisation that does not have much time or resources to audit invoices?

   A.   Fixed Price.

   B.   Time and Materials.

   C.   Cost Plus Incentive Fee.

   D.   Cost Plus Award Fee.

9. Which of the following takes place during the Conduct Procurements process?

   A.   Make-or-buy decisions.

   B.   Bidder conferences.

   C.   Source selection criteria.

   D.   Development of Procurement SOW.

10. Which of the following is NOT an advantage in a de-centralised contracting environment?

   A.   The procurement manager has more loyalty to the project.

   B.   The project manager has easier access to the procurement manager since they are part of the same team.

   C.   The procurement manager has a deeper understanding of the project and its needs since he is part of the project team.

D. The procurement manager can return to the procurement department after the project is complete.

11. You are negotiating with a potential customer to sell your company's flagship billing product. After many rounds of discussions, you have offered a final price of $530,000 that includes both product cost and complete professional service fee for deploying the product at customer premises. The customer's negotiator responds stating, "Sorry, I have been authorised to spend a maximum of $500,000 only. If you could reduce the final price to that amount, we will issue the purchase order within a week." What type of negotiating tactic is the negotiator using here?

A. Deadline.

B. Limited authority.

C. Missing man.

D. Delay.

12. In a Time and Materials contract, what is the biggest advantage a seller has?

A. The seller's profit is included in each hour of work.

B. The seller's profit is not known to the buyer.

C. The contract duration is brief.

D. The seller has an incentive to control cost.

13. You are a construction project manager who needs specialised heavy machinery for your next project that has a planned duration of one year. When you carry out a make-or-buy analysis, you get to know the following: the cost of buying the machinery is $24,000, the resale price of the machinery is one-third of the buy price, and the rental rate of the machinery

is $2000 per month. What should you do? Choose the best option.

    A.   Either buy or rent; both are equally viable as the costs will be the same for one year.

    B.   Unless the project can be completed in 8 months or less, the cheaper option is to buy.

    C.   If the project gets delayed, it will be cheaper to rent.

    D.   If the project can be completed a month early, it will be less expensive to rent.

14. In a Cost Plus Incentive Fee contract, the target cost was fixed at $500,000, the incentive fee was set at $25,000 and the buyer/seller sharing ratio was set at 80/20. However, the project was completed at just $450,000, well within the target cost. What was the final price paid by the buyer?

    A. $485,000

    B. $525,000

    C. $475,000

    D. $495,000

15. If a buyer submits an invitation to bid for purchasing industry standard materials for a construction project, what responses can the buyer expect from sellers?

    A.   Seller offers which are similar enough for the buyer to make a selection based on a seller's price.

    B.   Generic information about the sellers' capability to provide the necessary product or service.

    C.   Seller offers that are significantly different both in the solution approach and in price.

D. Individual responses from sellers asking for more information.

16. A buyer organisation is considering various contract options for entering into a contract with a seller and is likely to decide on a Cost Plus Award Fee (CPAF) contract. Which of the following statements is true for such contracts?

A. Payment of the award fee is decided by the customer based on satisfaction of performance criteria.

B. The award fee payment is linked to objective performance criteria.

C. Any unresolved dispute over the award fee is always subject to appeal in a court of law.

D. Performance criteria linked to award fee is captured in informal written communication.

17. As part of a requirement for a construction project, you need to purchase 100 tonnes of cement from a supplier. In order to guarantee structural stability, the cement strictly needs to be of a particular high grade and quality. You haven't worked with this supplier before and need to do a quality and grade inspection of the cement purchased to see if this meets specifications. However, conducting such a test will also mean wastage of a portion of the cement which you are purchasing at a high price. What is the best approach in this situation?

A. Skip the inspection and trust the supplier to have provided cement as per specifications.

B. Ask the supplier to provide a certificate of assurance for grade and quality.

C. Conduct the test on 10% of the delivered cement, and if the cement is found to meet specifications, order another 10% to make up for the cement wasted in testing.

D. Negotiate a contract with the supplier to provide more than 100 tonnes of cement, and conduct an acceptance testing on the surplus cement on delivery.

18. In which of the following instances should a buyer prefer a Time and Materials contract over a Fixed Price contract?

A. When the scope has been clearly defined and there is no chance of any further additions to the scope.

B. When the project scope is being progressively elaborated for individual deliverables.

C. When the prices for the materials used on the project are expected to increase sharply.

D. When the supplier will be using subcontractors whose invoices will be reimbursed by the buyer.

19. Jennifer is a project manager who needs some office equipment for her project and has the option of either buying or leasing the equipment. The purchase cost of the equipment is $1000 and its daily maintenance cost is $10. The cost of leasing the equipment is $110 per day. In how many days will the cost of leasing the equipment equal the cost of purchasing and using the equipment?

A. 9 days.

B. 10 Days.

C. 20 Days.

D. 5 Days.

20. What is a project manager's role in the procurement process? Choose the BEST option.

A. He plays the role of the primary negotiator in any procurement.

B. He plays little or no role in the procurement process.

C. He ensures that necessary provisions to address risks are included in the contract.

D. He dictates terms to the procurement manager.

21. Which of the following is NOT needed to have a contract in place?

A. Acceptance of both parties.

B. The procurement SOW.

C. The buyer's and seller's signatures.

D. The seller's address.

22. A seller completes delivery of all the work specified in the contract as per specifications. Nevertheless, the buyer was not satisfied with the work and expressed dissatisfaction vocally. The contract, in this situation, is considered:

A. Complete.

B. Null and Void.

C. Breached.

D. Incomplete.

23. All of the below are true with respect to bidder conferences, EXCEPT:

A. Sellers do not receive preferential treatment.

B. All sellers receive the same procurement documents.

C. Question and answer sessions take place in an open forum.

D. All sellers get to meet separately with the buyer.

24. What is meant by the 'point of total assumption' with respect to procurement contracts?

A. It is a special condition laid forth in only Time and Materials contracts.

B. It is the price-point in a fixed price contract above which a seller has to bear all costs for a cost overrun.

C. It is the point at which a Cost Reimbursable contract becomes profitable to a seller.

D. It refers to any clause in a contract which is based on assumptions.

25. How does the Close Procurements process differ from the Close Project or Phase process?

A. The Close Procurements process takes place before the Close Project or Phase process.

B. The Close Procurements process can take place only once during the course of a project unlike the Close Project or Phase process.

C. The Close Procurements process requires no customer involvement.

D. The Closure Procurements process is a part of the Monitoring and Controlling process group while Close Project or Phase is a part of the Closing process group.

26. A project manager needs to outsource a particular project activity and is in the process of reviewing proposals from various sellers. However, when the project manager sought

advice from his team members, they were divided in their opinion on which seller should be awarded the contract. Which of the following can best help the project manager in deciding who to award the contract to?

    A. The request for proposal document.

    B. The procurement management plan.

    C. The source selection criteria.

    D. Procurement audits.

27. John had held meetings with a representative from a vendor organisation regarding a software product John's company had planned to purchase. The meetings included discussions on individual modules that were to be included in the product. However, many months later, when the final product was delivered, John realised that a few modules, which were part of the discussions, were missing. When he enquired with the representative from the vendor organisation, he was told these missing modules – though agreed to be included during discussions – were excluded because the subsequent contract did not mention them and therefore the vendor wasn't legally obliged to provide them. Is the vendor representative correct in his assertion?

    A. No, he is incorrect; both parties should comply with what they agreed on.

    B. He is fairly correct as both parties are only legally obliged to conform to what is signed off in the contract.

    C. He is incorrect because he's obliged to honour all discussions.

D. He is correct because the supplier always makes the final decision on what should be delivered to the buyer.

28. A consulting company signs a contract to provide testing resources for an Information Technology (IT) firm about to commence a strategically important project. The contract's terms and conditions require the seller to provide the necessary hardware to conduct the testing too, but the consulting company failed to provide the hardware within the stipulated date. What is the best course of action for the IT firm's project manager?

A. Suspend all work till the time the consulting firm provides the hardware.

B. Issue a default letter to the consulting firm.

C. File a letter of intent.

D. Cancel the contract with the consulting firm.

29. Which of the following takes place during the Plan Procurement Management process?

A. Proposal evaluation.

B. Bidder conferences.

C. Procurement negotiations.

D. Make-or-Buy decision making.

30. A telecommunications company is undergoing restructuring and has accordingly formed a new procurement department. Procurement personnel who had been previously assigned to specific projects teams have now become part of the procurement team. Going forward, project managers will need to go through this team for all their procurement needs.

What distinct advantage does this newly restructured contracting environment hold over the previous one?

A. Project managers will have easier access to procurement managers.

B. Procurement personnel will become more loyal to the project.

C. There will be increased expertise among the procurement team personnel.

D. There will be no 'home' for procurement personnel.

Knowledge Area 9 – Procurement Management: Solutions

1. Answer A. Fixed price contracts offer the least cost risk to the buyer since the fee is known upfront and there is no variable component in the price, unlike what it is with Cost Reimbursable or Time and Materials contracts.

2. Answer B. Contract negotiations take place in the Conduct Procurement process.

3. Answer C. The most probable reason for declining the funding outright would have been because the LOI is not a legally binding document which obliges the buyer to follow through with the order. In other words, the LOI on its own cannot guarantee future revenue for Jamie's organisation on the basis of which short-term loans could be awarded.

4. Answer B. A request for proposal (RFP) is a document that is an output of the Plan Procurement process.

5. Answer D. When dealing with single source suppliers, a buyer is least likely to get the best possible price because the suppliers know they are not competing with other suppliers and therefore would not be motivated to keep prices as low as possible.

6. Answer C. Negotiations are used in the Conduct Procurements process and not in the Control Procurements process.

7. Answer A. Code escrow agreements help protect the interests of both the buyer and the seller. In the event that the seller goes out of business, the code will be made available to the buyer for continuing support of the product. Otherwise, the code will remain in escrow. Trying to buy the company for one product would be overkill while forcing the company to sell the source code would be unethical. Since the product is unique, finding another supplier for that product is also unlikely.

8. Answer A. In a Fixed Price contract, the onus is on the seller to control costs as the total price was already determined beforehand. The buyer has little to gain by auditing invoices for Fixed Price contracts and can therefore skip invoice auditing for such contracts without any consequences.

9. Answer B. Bidder conferences take place in the Conduct Procurements process. All other choices given are part of the Plan Procurement process.

10. Answer D. In a de-centralised contracting environment, there is no procurement department. Therefore, a disadvantage of such an environment is that the procurement manager will not have a 'home' department to return to after the project is complete.

11. Answer B. The negotiator is using the 'limited authority' negotiating tactic, when he states he is not authorised to spend the mentioned amount.

12. Answer A. The biggest advantage for a seller in a T&M contract is that the seller's profit is included in every hour of work.

13. Answer B. The cost of renting the machinery for a year is $2000 x 12 = $24,000. The cost of buying the machinery and selling it at the end of the project is $24,000 – ($24,000/3) = $16,000. Therefore the net cost of buying the machinery is only $16,000, which is equal to the cost of renting the machinery for 8 months (ie. $2000 x 8). Therefore, unless the project can be completed in less than 8 months, buying the machinery is undoubtedly the better option.

14. Answer A. Since the project cost came to only $450,000, there was a saving of $50,000 of which 20% was due to the seller organisation. Therefore, the final price paid by the buyer = $450,000 (cost incurred) + $25,000 (fixed incentive fee) + 20% of savings (ie. 20% of $50,000) = $450,000 + $ 25,000 +$10000 = $485,000.

15. Answer A. The PMBOK (5th Edition) states that terms such as bid, tender or quotation are generally used when the seller selection decision is based on price (usually for buying commercial or standard items). Therefore, the seller offers are expected to be more or less similar with the variations in price being the differentiator.

16. Answer A. The PMBOK (5th Edition) elaborates that payment of the award fee in a CPAF contract is based on the satisfaction of certain broad subjective performance criteria defined and incorporated in a contract. The performance criteria are not objective and are generally not subject to appeals. Award fee details are captured in the contract and therefore fall under formal written communication.

17. Answer D. The best approach in this situation would be for you to negotiate with the supplier and sign a contract to provide more than the required 100 tonnes, and then conduct an acceptance testing using the surplus. This would ensure that you do not need to use a part of the cement for testing and then order a second load (which would be time consuming and not efficient). Blindly trusting the supplier and obtaining a certificate of assurance are not effective approaches.

18. Answer B. From the given options, the only instance in which it is advantageous to the buyer to go for a Time and Materials contract over a Fixed Price contract is when the project scope is being progressively elaborated. Opting for a Fixed Price contract when the project scope is not clear could result in additional change orders, which could turn out to be very expensive for the buyer.

19. Answer B. If 'X' equals the number of days by when the purchase and lease costs become equal, then: $110X = \$1000 + \$10X$. Therefore, $\$100X=\$1000$ and on solving, we can see that X=10 Days.

20. Answer C. The project manager needs to ensure that various provisions are included in the contract to manage project risks associated with procurement.

21. Answer D. The contract has to include the procurement SOW and the signatures of both parties. The 'acceptance of both parties' is just another way of stating 'signatures from both parties'. The seller's address is not required though to have a valid contract.

22. Answer A. If a seller completes the work as specified in the contract, then irrespective of customer satisfaction, the contract is considered complete.

23. Answer D. Bidder conferences are meetings in which all the potential sellers and the buyer are present together. In bidder conferences, all sellers have equal and non-preferential access to the buyer. Sellers do not get to meet separately with the buyer in bidder conferences.

24. Answer B. The 'point of total assumption' pertains to Fixed Price contracts; it is the price above which a seller bears all losses for a cost overrun.

25. Answer A. The Close Project or Phase process commences only after the project or phase is completed and deliverables are accepted, and any procurement also needs to be closed before the Close Project or Phase process is initiated. Both Close Procurements and Close Project or Phase processes can occur more than once in a project that has multiple procurements and multiple phases. Both processes require customer involvement for acceptance before closure. Lastly, both processes belong to the Closing process group.

26. Answer C. The primary tool which needs to be used when deciding on a particular seller is the source selection criteria.

27. Answer B. The representative's assertion is fairly correct because the vendor organisation is legally obliged to provide only those modules that were included and signed off in the actual contract.

28. Answer B. When the seller has not conformed to the agreement in the contract, they have defaulted and therefore the buyer must take action. The buyer will need to use formal written communication to inform the seller of the default and inform them to meet their contractual obligation as a first step.

29. Answer D. Make-or-Buy decision making takes place during the Plan Procurement Management process. All other activities mentioned are part of the Conduct Procurements process.

30. Answer C. The new restructured contracting environment is centralised and in centralised environments, there will be greater levels of expertise because the department's personnel will focus specially on procurement related activities. However, in a centralised contracting environment, a project manager will find it more difficult to get access to a procurement manager, and procurement personnel would have less loyalty to specific projects since they would be splitting time between various projects. Also, procurement personnel in centralised environments have a home – the procurement department.

Knowledge Area 10 – Stakeholder Management: Questions

1. Who is a stakeholder?

    A.   Any person who is involved in a project's activities.

    B.   Anyone who can negatively influence a project.

    C.   Anybody who can positively influence a project.

    D.   Any person who can impact/ be impacted by a project- either positively or negatively.

2. Stakeholder engagement is critical to project success. Which are the five levels of stakeholder engagement?

    A.   Unaware, resistant, neutral, supporting and leading.

    B.   Oblivious, opposing, collaborating, delegating and leading.

    C.   Inactive, passive, active, hyper-active and leading.

D. Forming, storming, norming, performing and adjourning.

3. Which of the following is a tool/technique used by project managers to gather information about people whose interests need to be taken into account for any given project?

   A. Plan Stakeholder Management.

   B. Stakeholder analysis.

   C. Identify Stakeholders.

   D. Engage stakeholders.

4. Which of the following is not a constituent of the stakeholder management plan?

   A. Stakeholder management strategy.

   B. Scope and impact of change to stakeholders.

   C. Information to be distributed to stakeholders.

   D. List of issues identified during stakeholder engagement.

5. You are leading a project to implement a new CRM system in your organisation. However, the Support Team manager, whose team has been using the previous CRM for many years, has been vocally opposing the project and is against the implementation of the new CRM. This is despite the fact that this manager and his team are supposed to be among those who are expected to use the new CRM the most. What is the engagement level of the Support Team manager?

   A. Neutral.

   B. Resistant.

C.   Unaware.

D.   Supportive.

6. Dan is the project manager of a project that is in the 'Executing' phase. The project is running on schedule and as per the project management plan. At this juncture, a key stakeholder – a functional manager, approaches Dan confidentially and requests him to bypass the formal process to include a requirement that was missed in the requirements gathering stage. The functional manager promises Dan that if Dan were to include this change, he would reciprocate accordingly and return the favour someday. What should Dan do?

A.   Dan should agree to the request after the functional manager removes any part of the requirement that could affect the project's schedule or cost.

B.   Dan should conduct an impact assessment on the requested change and then submit it to the CCB.

C.   Dan should reject the request as he is not authorised to make any changes at this stage of the project.

D.   Dan should agree to the request since the functional manager is very likely to return the favour in future and doing so would also help in maintaining a good relationship.

7. A senior Vice-President of your organisation keeps calling you frequently to know the progress of your project because the project's outcome will impact his entire department of over 400 people. Which strategy should be used to manage a stakeholder who holds a place in the power interest grid like this VP?

A.   Manage closely.

B. Keep satisfied.

C. Keep informed.

D. Monitor.

8. Which of the following is not a classification model used for stakeholder analysis?

A. Power/interest grid.

B. Power/influence grid.

C. Potential/influence grid.

D. Salience model.

9. Which of the following is not a tool/technique of the Manage Stakeholder Engagement process?

A. Expert judgement.

B. Communication methods.

C. Interpersonal skills.

D. Management skills.

10. What is the primary output of the Identify Stakeholders process?

A. Stakeholder management plan.

B. Stakeholder register.

C. Project management plan.

D. Work performance data.

11. What is the term used to describe the degree to which a stakeholder can positively or negatively affect a project?

A. Level of interest.

B. Level of commitment.

C. Level of influence.

D. Level of conformance.

12. Amy took over a project from a project manager who had quit her organisation. Following the first status meeting after her takeover, Amy realised some key stakeholders had not been included in status meetings. There are also other key stakeholders who believe the project is futile and want to see it terminated. Which of the following documents should Amy first create to address these problems?

A. Status report.

B. Performance report.

C. Risk register.

D. Stakeholder register.

13. If a stakeholder has been plotted on the power/interest grid as high interest and low power, what would be the best approach for engaging him/her?

A. Keep the stakeholder informed of all project decisions and of any project update.

B. Closely manage his/her requirements and expectations.

C. Simply monitor and see if he/she requests for something and then act.

D. Give him/her complete responsibility of a project deliverable.

14. Amit's project team is located in South Asia though his customer is based in the US. The customer team head has requested Amit to send the weekly project status report to his US-based team by 9:00 am, Eastern Time, every Monday. This is an example of:

    A.   A stakeholder goal.

    B.   A stakeholder requirement.

    C.   A stakeholder expectation.

    D.   Decoded communication.

15. Which of the following details are NOT included in a stakeholder register?

    A.   Stakeholder contact information.

    B.   Stakeholder requirements.

    C.   Stakeholder name.

    D.   Stakeholder deliverables.

16. In which all project management process groups can stakeholders be identified?

    A.   Initiating and Planning.

    B.   Initiating, Planning, Executing, and Monitoring and Controlling.

    C.   Initiating, Planning and Closing.

    D.   Planning and Monitoring and Controlling.

17. Which of the following is NOT the responsibility of a project manager?

A. Enquiring with stakeholders about their expectations and requirements.

B. Obtaining stakeholder sign-offs after finalising requirements.

C. Creating the stakeholder register.

D. Selecting all the stakeholders for a project.

18. Robin has been designated as the project manager for an upcoming project. When she goes through the process of identifying various stakeholders, she realises that a functional manager, who has a reputation of being pedantic, and who is notorious for requesting numerous changes on any project he participates in, is a key stakeholder. What would be the best way for Robin to manage this situation?

A. Robin should exclude this stakeholder from communications as much as possible.

B. Robin should ask the functional head to move the stakeholder to a different role in the project.

C. Robin should get this stakeholder involved in the project as early as possible.

D. Robin should reject outright any changes requested by this stakeholder to dissuade him from submitting changes.

19. Which document captures details of a stakeholder's preferred communication method?

A. Stakeholder management plan.

B. Stakeholder register.

C. Stakeholders Engagement Assessment Matrix.

D. RACI matrix.

20. Which of the following details can be obtained from the Stakeholders Engagement Assessment Matrix?

A. The current level of engagement of a stakeholder.

B. The skill levels of each stakeholder.

C. The relationship between stakeholders.

D. The communication needs of a stakeholder.

21. Your monthly project meeting includes both internal and external stakeholders. Who of the following is not an internal stakeholder?

A. Project Team.

B. Program Manager.

C. Supplier.

D. Management.

22. The Manage Stakeholder Engagement process can result in all of the following, EXCEPT?

A. Documentation of lessons learned.

B. Change requests.

C. Updates to issue logs.

D. Work performance information.

23. Darren is the sponsor of an upcoming large ERP implementation project. He makes it a point to meet each of the major stakeholders in the project and request their support in

making the project a success. What is the engagement level Darren is displaying?

A. Resistant.

B. Unaware.

C. Leading.

D. Supportive.

24. An information management system allows a project manager to consolidate reports and facilitate report distribution to stakeholders. In which process is this tool used?

A. Identify Stakeholders.

B. Plan Stakeholder Management.

C. Manage Stakeholder Engagement.

D. Control Stakeholder Engagement.

25. You have been assigned as the project manager of a large project and you get to know this project has over 150 potential stakeholders. What should you ideally do in this situation?

A. You need to discard some of the stakeholders.

B. You need to gather the needs of only the important stakeholders.

C. You need to check with the sponsor to know who the important stakeholders are.

D. You should find an effective way to gather the needs of all stakeholders.

Knowledge Area 10 – Stakeholder Management: Solutions

1. Answer D. Stakeholders are those who can impact or be impacted by a project, either negatively or positively.

2. Answer A. The five levels of stakeholder engagement are: unaware, resistant, neutral, supporting and leading.

3. Answer B. Stakeholder analysis is a technique used by project managers to gather information about people whose interests need to be taken into account for any given project. It is used in the Identify Stakeholders process.

4. Answer D. The list of issues identified during stakeholder engagement is added to the Issue Log and is not included in the stakeholder management plan.

5. Answer B. The Support Team manager is aware of the project and its potential impact and is resistant to change; his level of engagement is, therefore, 'resistant'.

6. Answer B. This question has more to do with ethics than stakeholder management. Dan will need to follow the formal change control process to take this forward. Accordingly, he should conduct an impact analysis and then formally submit the change to the Change Control Board.

7. Answer A. This Vice-President can be categorised as a high-interest, high-power stakeholder on the power interest grid. Such stakeholders need to be managed closely.

8. Answer C. Potential/influence grid is not a real classification model while all the others are legitimate classification models.

9. Answer A. Expert judgement is not a tool/technique of the Management Stakeholder engagement process while all other three options are.

10. Answer B. The stakeholder register is the primary output of the Identify Stakeholders process. Other options provided are not outputs of this process.

11. Answer C. The correct term is 'level of influence'. The level of influence of a stakeholder depends on several factors such as the person's seniority, designation and status within an organisation.

12. Answer D. Amy should first create the stakeholder register and include details of all stakeholders in it. In this document, she also needs to capture the requirements and perspectives of the resistant stakeholders who want to terminate the project because doing so would make them less resistant or supportive once they realise that the project captures their needs and will address those too.

13. Answer A. Stakeholders who fall in the high interest and low power quadrant of the power/interest grid need to be kept informed of project activities and updates.

14. Answer C. This is an example of a stakeholder's expectation and should be ideally captured in the stakeholder register.

15. Answer D. Stakeholder deliverables are not included in a stakeholder register. All other options denote details which are included in the stakeholder register.

16. Answer B. Stakeholders can be identified throughout a project's duration. It is more beneficial and cost effective to identify them as early as possible though.

17. Answer D. Stakeholders are not selected by the project manager. People become stakeholders, by default, when their interests are affected positively or negatively by a project or/and when they can positively or negatively influence that project. A project manager only needs to identify stakeholders.

18. Answer C. The best option here is to involve the stakeholder as early as possible in the project. This would result in the stakeholder's requests getting captured early during the planning process, could help in avoiding rework, and will impact the project the least. It would not be advisable to reject changes requested because they could be genuinely needed for the project. Excluding the stakeholder from communications would only increase the likelihood of changes coming up late in the project where they can have a bigger impact. Asking for the stakeholder to be moved to a different role is simply a way of avoiding a problem instead of addressing it.

19. Answer A. The communication needs/requirements of a stakeholder are captured in the stakeholder management plan.

20. Answer A. The Stakeholders Engagement Assessment Matrix shows both the current and desired levels of engagement of a stakeholder.

21. Answer C. External stakeholders are those who are external to the (your) organisation. In this case it is the supplier who is the external stakeholder.

22. Answer D. Work performance information is an output of the Control Stakeholder Engagement process and is not an output of the Manage Stakeholder Engagement process.

23. Answer C. Darren is actively taking the initiative of meeting stakeholders to obtain their support for the project. He is in a 'leading' engagement role.

24. Answer D. An information management system is a tool used in the Control Stakeholder Engagement process.

25. Answer D. It is important to understand the needs of all stakeholders early in the project to organise it better and to prevent rework or changes late into the project. Therefore, you need to find a way to effectively gather the needs of all these stakeholders.

Professional Ethics: Questions

1. For which of the following teams is it most important to understand key cultural similarities and differences among team members?

   A. A team that is working on a project which is behind schedule and over budget.

   B. A co-located team having members with negligible socio-cultural differences.

   C. A cross-cultural globally dispersed team.

   D. A small team with less than 10 team members.

2. PMP practitioners are expected to show respect toward people and resources at all times. Which of the following is NOT an aspirational standard for practitioners in the global project management community?

   A. Practitioners need to keep themselves informed of norms and customs of others and avoid engaging in behaviour that might be considered disrespectful.

B. Practitioners are expected to listen to others' points of view and should seek to understand them.

C. Practitioners are expected to directly approach persons with whom they have a disagreement or conflict.

D. Practitioners are expected to conduct themselves in a professional manner, unless in situations where professionalism is not reciprocated.

3. One of your customers gifts you 2 tickets for an NFL game for which you had earlier tried to obtain tickets unsuccessfully. Each ticket costs $100 and the customer sent these to you as a token of appreciation for completing a recent project of theirs successfully. As per the existing code of conduct within your organisation, any employee who receives gifts that exceed $100 in value from a customer should immediately inform his/her designated H.R representative about the same. The H.R team will then accordingly make a decision on whether the gifts can be accepted after considering internal customer policies. What should you do?

A. Since the price of one ticket is $100, it is not above the allowed limit, and therefore you can accept the gift without informing your H.R representative.

B. You have received a gift that exceeds the allowed limit and therefore, you need to inform your H.R representative about it.

C. You can accept the gift and need not inform the H.R representative because the code of conduct is not applicable for management personnel.

D. You can accept the tickets, attend the game and later inform your H.R representative – this way you fulfil your ethical obligation and also get to watch the game.

4. The resource management team in your organisation has sent you the resumes of 5 candidates for you to consider for your project team. You check the online social-media profiles of the candidates to know them better and notice that one candidate is ostensibly very religious and has even quoted from a religious book in his profile. There is a lot of negativity associated with this person's religion and therefore you feel uncomfortable in having this candidate in your team. What should you do?

- A. Evaluate this candidate only on his suitability for the project role irrespective of his religious affiliation and then decide whether to accept or reject him.

- B. Reject the candidate because you feel that his religious views will conflict with that of others in your team.

- C. Since you believe the candidate's religious beliefs can be a problem, look for other candidates, and accept this candidate only if you are left with no other option.

- D. Reject the candidate because you feel uncomfortable but inform the HR you are rejecting him only because he doesn't have sufficient experience.

5. You need to depute one team member to an overseas client location to carry out an important activity for your project. There are two candidates who are equally capable of carrying out the activity and both are equally interested in the opportunity. However, you enjoy a far better personal rapport with one team member than you do with the other. What should you do?

- A. Choose the person you are closer with because the personal rapport you share with him will benefit the project.

- B. Choose the person you are less close with so that you can't be accused of favouritism.

C. Disclose the situation to these stakeholders and arrive at a joint decision.

D. Choose a third team member; even though he may not be as qualified as the other two; this will avoid needless conflict.

6. You are the project manager running a major construction project, and as a part of this project you have signed contracts with some vendor organisations. During the course of the project you get undeniable proof that an individual from one of the vendor organisations had received a substantial bribe to subcontract some work the vendor organisation is carrying out as part of your project. What should you do?

A. Ignore what you heard since this doesn't cost your organisation anything.

B. Quit this project and move to another project in your organisation so that you stay clear of any problems.

C. Report this incident to your management and to the management of your vendor organisation for them to take necessary actions.

D. Don't take any action for now, but ensure that your project work doesn't get hampered in any way.

7. You had completed all deliverables, as per agreed scope, for an office refurbishment project carried out for a government organisation. Nevertheless, you were not getting acceptance for deliverables from a stakeholder – a government official who neither responds to phone calls or emails. Finally, when you meet this official in private, he says, "I will provide you a sign-off, though in return you will need to pay me a minor fee which cannot be acknowledged officially." What should you do?

A. Pay the money so that you can get the acceptance.

B. Decline the offer from the official and report the incident to the management.

C. Pay the money only if the official provides a provisional sign-off first.

D. Negotiate with the official to reduce the 'fee' proposed by the official before agreeing.

8. You are about to attend a meeting in which you will present the weekly status report of your project to key stakeholders. Your project is running as per schedule and without any major issues so far and your report reflects this. Less than an hour before you get into the meeting, a quality engineer rushes in and informs you their team detected a major fault that might have a serious impact on the project schedule. It is too late to cancel/move the meeting at this stage and will need to go ahead with it. What should you do?

A. Present the weekly status report as it was already prepared, without informing the latest news to the stakeholders. Once the meeting is over, take steps to address the problem and following that, inform the stakeholders.

B. Present the weekly status report but also inform the stakeholders of the new issue, and provide them with a timeframe by when they will be updated about it, after due analysis is complete.

C. Attend the meeting and inform the stakeholders that the project has been delayed by a week.

D. Inform the quality engineer to recheck the fault and update you after the meeting; proceed to the meeting and present the weekly status report as originally planned.

9. A project manager has been informed by his Quality Lead that one of the last deliverables awaiting acceptance from the customer before project closure has been found to have a minor defect. The customer is unlikely to identify this defect because the deliverable meets the contract requirement even though it doesn't meet internal quality standards of the project manager's organisation. What should be the project manager's next course of action in this situation?

- A. He should await the customer's acceptance and then proceed for closure; post closure, he should inform the Maintenance and Support team to rectify the defect.

- B. He needs to record details of this defect in the lessons learned for future reference.

- C. He should inform the customer that the project will be delayed.

- D. He should discuss the issue with the customer.

10. While carrying out a last-minute review of a project status report, a project manager realised one of his project team members had been fudging numbers and had significantly over-reported the number of hours she spent on the project; this has in turn skewed the project statistics. What should the project manager do first and foremost in this situation?

- A. Report the team member's action to her functional manager.

- B. Revise the report and send it across with only accurate project statistics and information.

- C. Speak with the team member to discuss the impact of her action.

- D. Send the report as it is for now and then address the problem in the next report.

11. You have organised a meeting with a supplier organisation's representatives for contract negotiations related to deliverables of an upcoming project. However, a day before the negotiations are scheduled to take place, the project sponsor informs you the project might get cancelled because the COO has come up with a proposal for another strategic project using the funds earmarked for your project. What should you do?

    A. Inform the supplier's representatives that all negotiations have been cancelled.

    B. Go ahead with the meeting anyway.

    C. Go ahead with the meeting but only discuss important deliverables.

    D. Postpone negotiations.

12. You are managing a project to implement your company's flagship product at your customer's premises. While the project is in progress, your company's Product Roadmap team releases some new product upgrades which were not expected for another 6 months. The upgrades comprise product functionality which the customer had requested for at the beginning of the project but which was not available at the time of the project commencement. What should you do?

    A. Since a change request wasn't issued by the customer, simply continue as planned.

    B. Communicate with the customer on the availability of the upgrades and the impact it could have on project constraints were it to be included.

    C. Include the upgrades as part of the project since it was an original ask.

D. Continue as per current plan and after project completion, inform the customer of the upgrades, so that the upgrades can be taken up as a separate project.

13. Your company has received responses from various suppliers for an RFP that was floated in order to purchase some specialised software. You are part of the team evaluating the supplier responses and you realise one of the proposals came from the organisation owned by your cousin. Your cousin has been somebody who has helped you in the past and he would expect a favourable response from you. What should you do?

A. You should support the proposal by your cousin's company as you know he's a man of integrity and because you believe his organisation will be a reliable supplier.

B. You should disclose your relationship with the supplier to your management and opt out of the selection team.

C. You should go ahead and support the proposal by your cousin's company if suppliers had been previously chosen on account of such relationships.

D. You should move out of the selection team but should strongly recommend your cousin's organisation to those in the selection team as there's no wrong in that.

14. Your management usually asks you to reduce project cost estimates by 15% every time you submit the estimate for a new project. You are due to submit the cost estimate for a new project to the management team later this week. What should you do this time?

A. Pad up the cost estimates by over 15% so that even if management asks you to cut 15% of the estimates, the revised estimates will match what you actually planned for.

B. Identify an area where 15% savings can be achieved by the project.

C. Provide an accurate estimate of the costs along with the data to support the estimate.

D. Cut 15% from your actual cost estimate and then submit it to the management.

15. James is a PMP certified project manager who has been contacted by PMI for some information regarding another PMP certified project manager who was reported to be a participant in some unethical activities. The other project manager is James' colleague and friend and James is aware of his colleague's involvement in the mentioned unethical activities. Responding to PMI with the requested information is likely to result in the suspension of his friend's PMP credentials. What should James do?

A. James should ignore PMI's request; it is not mandatory to respond to such enquiries.

B. James should cooperate and provide the necessary information to PMI.

C. James should respond to PMI denying any knowledge of the mentioned activities.

D. James should respond to PMI but decline to provide the requested information because doing so would jeopardise his relationship with his friend.

16. You read a famous management book written by a well-known management guru and found the knowledge you gained from one particular chapter in the book especially useful. You

would like to share this knowledge with your team members. What should you do?

A. Scan the useful chapter of the book using the office scanner and distribute it to team members via email.

B. Take photocopies of the useful chapter from the book and distribute the copies to your team members.

C. Have a candid discussion with your team members to let them know about the book and about the knowledge you gained from it, and then encourage them to buy their personal copies too.

D. Find a website from where free pirated PDF copies of the book can be downloaded and forward your team members the link.

17. You work for an organisation that operates mostly in the Telecommunication domain. Recently, your company completed its first banking project and you were the project manager who had managed the project. Though, the project had many challenges, you learned a lot from it and you now have significant knowledge on how to manage similar projects in future. How should you BEST leverage this knowledge?

A. Use the knowledge to showcase your eligibility for similar new projects in your company.

B. Find a new company that can pay you better since your newfound knowledge and experience is valued highly by other employers too.

C. Ask for a raise or promotion because you're the only project manager who has management experience in that domain in your organisation.

D. Discuss with your management to conduct training sessions to equip others in your organisation with your newly acquired knowledge and experience.

18. You have organised a week-long training activity in one of your offices. The training is also attended by some of your overseas team-members who have travelled to your country for the first time. After the completion of the training, all team-members were asked to join for some informal team-building activities. However, when the team-building activities commence, you notice that two of the overseas team-members refuse to take part in the activities stating that such activities are in conflict with the socio-religious practices in their country. What should you ideally do in such a situation?

A. Excuse the two team-members from participation and ensure that any such activities planned in the future are more inclusive and do not conflict with socio-religious beliefs of participating team-members.

B. Insist that the two team-members participate for only a short while so that they do not end up being spoilsports.

C. Tell the team members that these team-activities are completely acceptable in the local culture and hence, they should also learn to adapt to the local culture and participate.

D. Excuse the team-members from participation but report to their functional managers about their non-cooperation.

19. You have to choose between 2 suppliers for purchasing certain product components in bulk. The component specifications are of a global standard and hence, there is little to choose between the suppliers in terms of quality and the only differentiator is the price offered by the suppliers. You decide to finalise the supplier offering the lower price, when

you get to know this supplier employs illegal immigrants and pays them less than prescribed minimal wages to save costs. What should you do?

- A. Sign the contract with the supplier offering lower costs; what happens in their factories is not your concern.

- B. Refuse to work with the lower priced supplier and choose the other supplier instead.

- C. Consult your manager on which supplier to choose.

- D. Sign the contract with the lower cost supplier if your company has no legal liability for any of their actions.

20. In a recent team meeting, one of your team members cracked a racist joke which was met with laughter by most people in the room and with indifference by a few others. Though you don't approve of what he did, the team member is a valuable resource and you do not want to get into a confrontation unnecessarily because that might affect your project. This was also the first time the team member said something of this sort. What should you do?

- A. Have a private meeting with the team member and explain to him that racist jokes are unacceptable.

- B. Ignore the incident as it was just a joke.

- C. Report the team member to this functional manager.

- D. Remove the team member from your project team.

Professional Ethics: Solutions

1. Answer C. Cultural differences often result in differences in language, cultural values, nonverbal actions and cultural practices. If team members do not know how to handle these differences, it could affect the project. Such differences are likely to arise in cross-cultural globally dispersed teams and therefore it is very important for such teams to understand key cultural similarities and differences.

2. Answer D. As outlined in the PMI Code of Ethics, practitioners in the global project management community are expected to conduct themselves in a professional manner at all times, even in situations where professionalism is not reciprocated.

3. Answer B. You were gifted 2 tickets valued cumulatively at $200 - this is above the threshold limit and you are ethically obliged to report this to your H.R representative immediately, as per the code of conduct.

4. Answer A. The PMI Code of Ethics and Conduct specifies that practitioners of project management should not discriminate others on gender, race, age, religion, disability, nationality, or sexual orientation. Therefore, the candidate should be evaluated solely on his suitability for the project role irrespective of what his religious beliefs are.

5. Answer C. This is a situation in which there is a conflict of interest. As per the PMI Code of Ethics and Conduct, any potential conflict of interest should be fully disclosed to appropriate stakeholders and the PM practitioner should refrain from the decision making process, unless or until: a full disclosure is made to the affected stakeholders, an approved mitigation plan is in place, and the consent of the stakeholders has been obtained to proceed.

6. Answer C. As a project manager, you have the ethical responsibility of informing your management and the party affected of this misdeed. Withholding information about unethical practices is considered unethical too.

7. Answer B. The official is asking for a bribe and payment of any amount of bribe, under any condition, is unethical. You need to decline the offer, and report the incident to your management.

8. Answer B. Withholding information from stakeholders is considered an unethical action. You will need to proceed to the meeting and inform that stakeholders of the recent development and then provide them a timeframe by when you can update them after conducting due analysis. Asking the quality engineer to simply go and re-check the fault and report it again after the meeting is just an 'avoidance' technique.

9. Answer D. The project manager should discuss the issue with the customer and then decide how to go ahead. Withholding information from the customer would be unethical and is therefore incorrect. Delaying the project might result in contract breach and would be a premature decision if other viable alternatives can be discussed with the customer. Lastly, simply recording the details in lessons learned doesn't address the problem.

10. Answer B. The project manager's first priority here is to accurately represent the project data in the status report that is due. He should not send misrepresented information intentionally as that would be unethical. Following this, he will need to discuss with the team member about her actions and if that action does not yield results, the project manager should report the team member's behaviour to her functional manager.

11. Answer D. Since there is a possibility the project might get cancelled, the best option would be to postpone negotiations till the time there is certainty. Cancellation of negotiations would be a premature decision as the final decision on the project hasn't been made yet. Conducting the negotiations in part or full would result to wasted time and effort if the project were to be cancelled.

12. Answer B. Since the customer had asked for the functionalities that are present in the new upgrades, it would be unethical to withhold the information about the availability of these upgrades. However, these cannot be included by default in the project because doing so might have cost/schedule impacts on the project and such an inclusion has to go through the change process. The right thing to do first would be to inform the customer of the availability of the upgrades and any potential impacts it could have, were it to be included as part of the current project, for them to make an informed decision on whether they should raise a change request to include these upgrades as part of the on-going project.

13. Answer B. A project manager of the global project management community should apply the rules of the organisation without favouritism or prejudice. Directly supporting your cousin's company or even trying to influence the selection is a show of favouritism. You should inform your management about the conflict of interest and volunteer to move out of the selection team to ensure that fair assessments are made of the proposals floated by all suppliers without any bias.

14. Answer C. A project manager is ethically bound to create an accurate estimate and stand by it. Padding is unethical whereas identifying where savings can be achieved doesn't address the problem. Submitting an estimate that's understated will result in a cost override. The right option is to create an accurate estimate and justify the estimate with supporting data. If management still needs to cut costs, they will then need to look at other alternatives.

15. Answer B. PMI's code of Ethics and Professional Conduct requires a project manager to report unethical behaviour and violations of the code. As a PMP certified project manager, James is obliged to cooperate with the PMI in collecting information. By ignoring the PMI's request, or by falsely denying knowledge of the unethical conduct, or by declining PMI's request, James would not be complying with the code himself.

16. Answer C. Scanning/Photocopying and distributing, or even providing links to download pirated free PDF copies of copyrighted property is unethical, and sometimes, even illegal. You should not copy or distribute material from copyrighted material. The right thing to do is to speak with your team members, share your experience and encourage them to purchase their own copies.

17. Answer D. Project managers should strive to contribute to the project management community and to the Project Management Body of Knowledge. Conducting training sessions to share knowledge with others is one of the ways in which this can be achieved. All other options refer to personal gains only.

18. Answer A. The best course of action in the situation is to excuse the team members from participation and to ensure that any future activities are more inclusive in nature and not in conflict with socio-religious beliefs of any participating team-members – this shows a healthy respect for cultural differences. Lodging a complaint against the team-members or forcing them to take part in activities they are clearly uncomfortable with shows a disrespect for cultural differences.

19. Answer B. You should not condone or assist others engaging in illegal or unethical behaviour and this is clearly what the supplier offering lower costs is doing. Therefore, the right thing to do is to refuse to work with such a supplier and to opt for the other supplier even though you have to pay a higher price.

20. Answer A. Discharging the team member or reporting him would be excessive penalty for a first time offence. However, it is not something to be ignored either because such behaviour is disrespectful. The team member should therefore be met with in private and told that such behaviour is unacceptable and that he shouldn't indulge in it thereafter.

A Final Note

I have said this before and will say it again. Passing the PMP is not a herculean task. But it is something that requires discipline, dedication, focussed effort and patience.

In addition to the practice questions in this book, and the end-of-chapter questions you would have practised on while studying for the PMP exam, you need to also spend some time attempting full length mock tests to help you prepare for the exam. Sitting for 4 hours at a stretch attempting 200 questions is physically and mentally exhausting and you will need to get used to working out questions for such long durations to prepare yourself for the actual exam.

Disclaimer: Through this book, I have put in my best effort to bring you a set of well-planned and carefully compiled set of practice questions which give you a fair amount exposure to the kind of questions to expect on the PMP. Nevertheless, this should not be interpreted as a promise or guarantee for your success. Your efforts should stretch far beyond the boundaries of this book. Any positive or negative outcome is ultimately dependent on your capability, wholehearted commitment and the overall effort you put into your exam preparation.

Your Feedback is Valuable

Did you like this book and find it useful?

If yes, I would really appreciate it if you could let other readers know by posting a short review. It does not matter if your review is written in a few lines or in just a few words. Your gesture will help give this book the much needed exposure in a crowded market place.

You can post your review on Amazon.com by navigating to this website link: https://www.amazon.com/dp/B01NCEMV9N/

About the Author

Roji Abraham is a PMP certified Project Manager who works for a leading Information Technology (IT) organisation in India. He holds a Bachelor's Degree in Electronics and Communication Engineering and an M.B.A degree from Warwick Business School, UK.

After commencing his professional career in 2004, he has worked exhaustively in client service roles and has spent most of his time since 2009 managing projects, teams, and delivering to Tier-1 IT clients in locations across Asia, Africa and Europe.

Roji also enjoys blogging and writing fiction, having published his maiden short story collection in 2015 titled 'Kaleidoscopic Lives. He maintains an active presence on social media and you can connect with him at the following social media locales:

Twitter: http://twitter.com/RojiAbraham1

Quora: https://www.quora.com/profile/Roji-Abraham

Facebook: http://facebook.com/authorrojiabraham

Official Author Website: https://rojiabraham.com

You can also contact Roji directly by sending an email to **author@rojiabraham.com**

Be A PMP Ace in 30 Days

Author Roji Abraham writes in his unique style about his 30 day journey to PMP certification and gives step-by-step guidance on how you could effectively utilise your time while preparing for the PMP Exam.

'Be a PMP ace in 30 days' isn't a full-fledged guide with a truckload of information on each section but rather, a companion book, that shows you, how in 30 days, you could use your resources effectively, and be ready for the PMP exam and succeed. That too, without having to take even a day off from work!

Here's what you get from this value-for-money book that will oversee your personal journey to PMP certification:

1. Guidance on the necessary tools and resources you need while preparing for the PMP exam and how to use them effectively.

195

2. A downloadable weekly calendar with suggested daily and hourly schedules for covering each topic and reviewing them effectively over 30 days.

3. A print-friendly downloadable process chart.

4. Key notes for each day that highlights the most important topics for that day.

5. Information on some great free/budget online resources.

6. Useful tips for the exam day.

7. Five interviews with successful PMP candidates, from around the globe, with their suggestions on how to conquer the PMP exam.

If you aim to get PMP certified, get this value-for-money pocket gem now.

To view more details about the book or to purchase the book on Amazon, navigate to this Amazon website link: https://www.amazon.com/dp/B018ZBVIU6.

Join the Monthly Newsletter

There is a monthly newsletter dispatched to subscribers of **rojiabraham.com** that provides information about the author Roji's latest blog posts, and details of upcoming titles.

This monthly newsletter will also contain the occasional goodies like free downloads or discounts on featured titles!

You can subscribe to the newsletter at this link: http://bitly.com/rojiabraham-newsletter

83223417R00114

Made in the USA
Lexington, KY
10 March 2018